WE NEVER WENT TO THE MOON

America's Thirty Billion Dollar Swindle

Bill Kaysing

PRINTING HISTORY
Mokelumne Hill Press edition published 1976
Saucerian Press edition published 1981
Society of Metaphysicians Ltd. edition published 1999
New Saucerian Press edition published 2017

Table Of Contents

Foreword

It has been estimated that about 30 per cent of the adult population of the United States does not believe that this country has landed astronauts on the moon. That's quite a percentage of boosters for this book before it is even published. Perhaps after it has been circulated there will be even more. And eventually, if Bill's theory is correct, 100 per cent of the entire world will know about one of the biggest hoaxes in the world's history.

While the moon swindle is gigantic, it actually takes a lesser place to such monstrous hoaxes as . . .

The Great 200 Billion Dollar Food Swindle!

The Giant 300 Billion Dollar Tax Swindle!

plus swindles perpetrated by the U.S. Government in the areas of defense spending, drugs, medicine, price rigging, social security and on and on, ad infinitum.

Our Cast of Characters . . .

AEC   Atomic Energy Commission
AF   Air Force
ASP   Apollo Simulation Project
CFR   Council on Foreign Relations
CIA   Central Intelligence Agency
DIA   Defense Intelligence Agency
LEM   Lunar Excursion Module
NAA   North American Aviation Corp.
NASA National Aeronautic and Space Administration
NSA   National Security Act
NSC   National Security Council
OSS   Office of Strategic Services

Introduction

"Apparently a substantial number of Americans do not believe that their government landed men on the moon", says David Wise in "The Politics Of Lying", 1973. On June 14, 1970, the Knight newspapers published an astonishing story based on interviews with 1,721 persons in six cities. The people interviewed were asked whether they really believed that U.S. astronauts had been to the moon and back.

The article emphasized that no attempt had been made to reach a cross section of the population. Nevertheless, the interviews did indicate that a substantial number of Americans do not believe the single most publicized action ever taken by their government in peacetime.

When the skeptics were asked why such an enormous hoax would be perpetrated, they generally replied either that the government had done it to fool the Russians and Chinese, or that it had been done to justify the great cost of the space program. A few thought the government had a bread-and-circuses motive to make the people forget their troubles.

Government deception, supported by a pervasive system of official secrecy and an enormous public relations machine, has reaped a harvest of massive public distrust.

Rocketdyne Division
6633 Canoga Avenue
Canoga Park, California 91304
Telex. 651488

Rockwell International

December 3, 1975

William Kaysing
146 Palo Verde Terrace
Santa Cruz, California 95060

Dear Mr. Kaysing:

Although we do not have copies of the termination papers you would have received when you left Rocketdyne, we can confirm the following information:

Hire Date: 02-13-1956, Technical Writer, Senior
Classification Change: 09-24-1956 - Service Analyst
Classification Change: 09-15-1958 - Service Engineer
Classification Change: 10-07-1962 - Publications Analyst
Quit - Personal Reasons: 05-31-63

We hope the above information will serve your purpose.

Very truly yours,

ROCKWELL INTERNATIONAL CORPORATION
Rocketdyne Division

F. Harnasch
Employee Relations

FH:kw

Kaysing has this letter to prove employment at Rocketdyne Division of Rockwell International and that he quit in 1963 for personal reasons.

CENTRAL INTELLIGENCE AGENCY
WASHINGTON, D.C. 20505

1 0 DEC 1975

Mr. Bill Kaysing
146 Palo Verde Terrace
Santa Cruz, CA 95050

Dear Mr. Kaysing:

Please excuse the long delay in answering your request. It was caused solely by the heavy crush of similar requests which descended on CIA this summer.

We have made a thorough search of our files and found some items pertaining to you. For your retention, I am enclosing one document, a Biographic Data Sheet of 27 October 1960.

Unfortunately, there are a number of other items which cannot be released. I am listing them below and alongside each item is the appropriate exemption from the Freedom of Information Act which gives the reason for their denial. I will explain the exemptions following the list.

Document	FOIA Exemptions
(1) Inter-Office memorandum, dated 8 December 1960.	
(2) Case Processing Record, dated 6 December 1960.	(b)(3), (b)(7)(E)
(3) Case Processing Record, dated 30 November 1960.	(b)(3), (b)(7)(E)
(4) Request for Contract Security Authorization, dated 7 February 1962.	(b)(3), (b)(7)(E)
(5) Security Approval Request from Chief, Security Staff/OL, dated 4 October 1960, with Biographic Data attached.	(b)(1), (b)(3)
	(b)(1), (b)(3)

The CIA has a file on Kaysing but refuses to release the information. What is it that is so secret?

Bill Kaysing was head of the Technical Presentations Unit at the Rocketdyne Propulsion Field Laboratory from 1956 until 1963. This period encompassed the major planning for the engine system and related components of the Apollo Project. During this time he was cleared for U.S. Air Force "Secret" and Atomic Energy "Q".

Author of several books on the subject of reducing or eliminating corporate control over an individual's life, Kaysing divides his time between travel in the Western United States and numerous writing stints aboard his boat in Northern California.

1

How This Book Came To Be Written

During the summer of 1969, I was living in a small house on the beach in Santa Barbara, California. A fanfare of newspaper stories heralded the launch of the astronauts to the moon. Soon, I knew, TV screens would flicker with barely discernible pictures of moon walkers.

But despite a seven year stint at Rocketdyne, the firm that built the main propulsion units for Apollo, I could not work up the least bit of interest in the entire astrophysical circus . . . not even to the extent of reading an article or watching the most exciting moments on the boob tube. Why, I wondered.

Why, of all people, shouldn't I be captivated with the prospect of seeing the fruition of my work and the labors of thousands of others who had contributed to the Apollo voyage programs. Why indeed?

I decided I did not believe that Armstrong, Collins and Aldrin or anyone else was going to the moon. And consequently, I could not generate the least enthusiasm for watching a phony performance.

From whence did this odd idea come, I wondered. I had not really given the Apollo program much thought in the years since leaving Rocketdyne. I had followed it in a cursory fashion, becoming aware of it only through the more startling developments: the fire on Pad 34, for example.

So it is possible that I had simply lost interest in astronautics despite the prospect of a moon landing. But I didn't think so; there was more to it than mere diminishment of interest. Somehow I seemed to have perceived that the Apollo project had become a gigantic hoax and that nobody was leaving earth for the moon, certainly not in July of 1969.

Call it a hunch, an intuition; information from some little understood and mysterious channel of communication . . . a metaphysical message. While tenuous and ephemeral at its source, it was strong and vivid in its form. In short, a true conviction.

I watched none of the moon "landings" nor did I pay much attention to print media presentations.

Since summer of 1969, the feeling and belief that a man's journey to the moon is still in his future became stronger. I paid even less attention to the follow-on "flights" of Apollo and noticed that many others were equally neglectful.

As the years passed, I found myself comparing the Apollo flights to many other incidents in American life. Watergate was an outstanding example and a striking point of comparison. Here was a case of leaders presenting one face to the public while another was completely hidden; a Machiavellian duplicity that has shocked many people and shattered their complacency.

The energy 'crisis' was another Apollo simulation. Here, an entire industry created an artificial shortage to ram the price increases down the throats of resisting but still gullible consumers.

But, as Lincoln so wisely said, you cannot fool all the people all the time. Thus, in many places, the facade of the corporate state began to crack. However, instead of apologies and excuses, a vicious arrogance appeared (the attitudes of Haldeman and Ehrlichman reflect this). Even in public relations-type advertising, an attitude of "take it or leave it" emerged from the formerly velvet-glove-over-the-mailed-fist corporations.

Now was the time to ask some questions of NASA regarding their Apollo program . . . questions that I found continually badgering my mind. Questions like, why didn't the astronauts make some visible signal from the moon? It would have been relatively easy to touch off some hypergolic chemicals, beam a laser to a mirror on earth, create a pattern

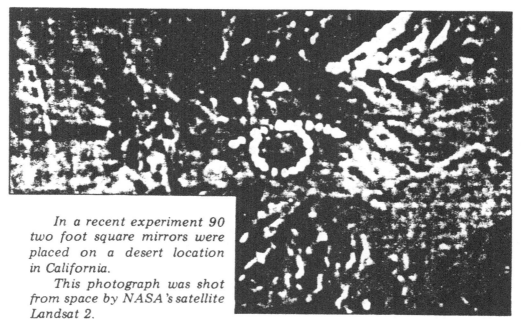

In a recent experiment 90 two foot square mirrors were placed on a desert location in California.

This photograph was shot from space by NASA's satellite Landsat 2.

Why was not something similar done on the moon? A lightweight reflective milar or tin foil could have been used and achieved the same results.

with lightweight black dust or provide some other means of definitely proving that they were really there. Relying on an easily simulated picture on TV was the least believable means of "proof".

Why did the Dutch papers, circa 1969, question the authenticity of the moon landing? And more importantly, why did the American press ignore the otherwise interesting sidelight?

Why is it that NASA's Apollo records are not classified, but are also not available to the general public? In a letter to me from the present head of technical publications of Rocketdyne, there is this comment: "Apollo material not classified but unavailable to the public . . ."

Why did so many astronauts end up as executives of large corporations? Was this their real reward for the moon 'trip'?

Why did some astronauts die in accidents, others suffer

brain damage and still others have nervous breakdowns? Was this rate of attrition higher than should be expected for this type of carefully selected and trained individual? Did it relate to the high incidence of departure of witnesses to the Kennedy murder?

What has happened to the Baron Report?—a 500 page compilation of errors, instances of mismanagement and malfeasance, written by Thomas Baron prior to the death of the three astronauts on Pad 34 in 1967. And was Baron's death a few months later at a railroad crossing really an accident?

Why did the relatives of astronauts so often refer to the unreality of events? Was it because the events really were unreal?

Why was the fact that the astronauts were training in the Las Vegas area not publicized? Every other aspect of their lives was examined in close detail. Was it because a part of the Nevada desert (specifically, the Mercury test site for AEC use) was being groomed as a moon "set"?

Why were the first astronauts held in quarantine so long after their 'trip' when most scientists agree that the moon is sterile and there was virtually no chance of disease transmission? Was it because the astronauts needed a period of reconditioning after the spurious trip? Was it because they simply could not bear to face hordes of cheering people so soon after playing roles in a show on earth?

Why was Apollo 6, a total fiasco, followed by six pefect moon missions which in turn were followed by the manned orbiting lab debacle? Doesn't this cause a credibility gap among both statisticians and laymen?

Why was there a rigid and unbending requirement that all data for public release be cleared through the public relations office of NASA?

Why were all transmissions to be public via TV and radio, media of communication easily faked? Why was there nothing to see other than the launch and some fuzzy pictures allegedly coming from the moon?

Is there any real assurance that the astronauts were

We Never Went To The Moon

Here's a photograph of the astronauts walking toward the Apollo Capsule . . . .

. . . . would you bet your life that they were in the Apollo Capsule when the rocket roared into space?

actually aboard the Apollo vehicle? Also, is there any proof that it really flew with a full load of fuel? Or did it make it off the pad because it was lightly and safely loaded with engines running at reduced power?

Eight astronauts died in non-space accidents: were they all accidents?

Why did Wernher Von Braun leave NASA to become a Fairchild executive? His whole life until then was devoted to space travel; in fact, he was obsessed. Did he finally realize the folly of trying to reach the moon with equipment built by the lowest bidder and the firms with the most skilled lobbyists?

What did Pat Collins mean by her remark on July 20th, 1969, 4:05 p.m. Houston time, when she declared, "It's about as real as anything about this whole thing is . . .", when she was asked if a simulation docking (as seen on TV) was real.

Why were the moon rocks rushed to Switzerland after they landed? What proof do we have that they are actually rocks from the moon?

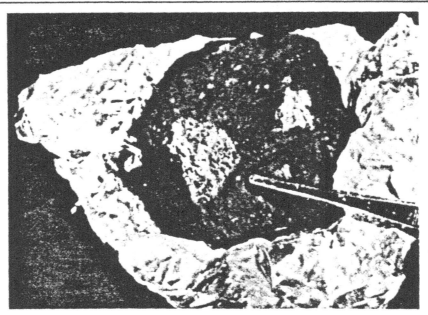

Of all the tasks undertaken to assure the near-success of the hoax, creation of believable moon rocks was the easiest. By their own admission, all rocks contained minerals common to earth; in short, no real surprises at all.

Here's an Apollo capsule returning to earth over 4 miles from the pickup carrier, disappearing well into the horizon on it landing.

Why did the landing of all Apollo return capsules take place out of sight of the public—and even of the pickup carrier crews?

Why was there never a mention of gold, silver, diamonds or other precious metals on the moon? Wasn't this a viable consideration? Why was this fact never discussed in the press or by the astronauts?

Why was the fact that the moon mission was really a military project concealed from the public? Many military fiascos are hidden from the public to avoid loss of prestige.

Many other questions similar to the above have never been satisfactorily answered by either NASA, the press or the scientists involved.

We invite an answer to these questions now. In fact, the entire book is an invitation to NASA or other groups or concerned individuals to review the concept presented and refute it with some indisputable evidence that we have, indeed, landed on the moon—that we have, indeed, made good use of the 30 billion dollars that allegedly went to fund Apollo.

Photos, ticker tape parades, a bag of rocks and other superficial items do not provide adequate answers to the questions posed above, or to those presented in the following chapters.

2

Why Go To The Moon?

"I believe that we are in a race and I have said many times, Mr. Webb . . . tell me how much money you need and this Committee will authorize all you need."
> —James Fulton, Congressman

To realize how important it was to ensure a successful "man on the moon" project, we must first examine the roots of the desire and need for this all-important flight.

Long before space became a factor in U.S.-Russia competition, other aspects of comparison were used by propagandists. For instance, comparisons were made to determine:

1. Amount of time spent by laborers to earn a specific amount of food.
2. Ownership of automobiles, houses and other big-tag items.
3. Female beauty: Russian women were usually shown wearing shawls and long skirts made of heavy burlap.

Thus, when competition is in science, specifically space flight became a factor in the battle for men's minds, no limits were imposed.

In other words, the U.S. became like a frantic gambler who sees ever-increasing losses threatening total disaster. Finally, he mortgages his house and children to make one last colossal bet. He MUST win or all is gone.

NOTE: It has been conjectured that the Soviets intended that a totally spurious race take place, knowing that the financial strains would contribute to a weakening of the U.S. financially and as a world power. However, this is not in keeping with the wheels-within-wheels concept that there is no real competition between the U.S. and Russia (or any other country, for the matter), since the ultimate manipulators are in league.

The Foundations Of Space Ventures In The U.S.

Little was done prior to WWII in the U.S. as far as space travel was concerned. Only Goddard and his lone-wolf experiments advanced the technology. As usual, the military was a decade or two late in recognizing an advanced weapon potential.

However, with the search for new death-dealing devices during WWII, rockets came under intensive research and development. Thus, when the German scientists were brought to this country in 1946, they were joined with the nucleus of a group that was to later create an entirely new scientific venture.

Early U.S. efforts employed the tested engines of the V-2 missile. The A-4 engine, as it was called, was the building block of such military missiles as Redstone and Thor. Finally, newer designs evolved into Atlas and Titan. The hardware for these military rockets became the platform on which the subsequent rocket systems were based. Unfortunately, as we have pointed out elsewhere, the choice was always in the liquid propellant engine area.

There is no question that the Russians have employed their efforts in rocketry as a propaganda tool. As Logsdon points out: "The Soviets have used technology as an instrument of propaganda and power politics as illustrated by their great and successful efforts and careful political timing in space exploration. They have sought constantly to present spectacular accomplishments in space as an index of national strength.

"The flight of Sputnik in 1957 was certainly an outstanding manifestation of this concept. It acted as a vigorous prod to U.S. peace efforts. As Lyndon Johnson said, in true shit-kick fashion: "I guess for the first time I started to realize that this country of mine might not be ahead of everything."

Soon, the laissez-faire doctrine of Eisenhower was reserved, by Johnson as Senate minority leader, and later by President Kennedy. NASA, which had been given the assignment for manned flight in space, was energized with personnel and money. The basis for the moon flight decision was now in existence.

3

Elements Of
Rocket Propulsion

The Chinese discovered rockets around 700 A.D. They used them for weapons and for celebrations. Early rockets such as the Chinese used, and later those used by the English for warfare, were solid propellant types. Not until the 20th Century was the possibility of using more efficient but more complex liquid propellant systems.

Robert Goddard, a lone-wolf American experimenter, pursued the science of liquid propelled rockets in the 1920's and early 1930's. He achieved most of the initial successes in this field. His efforts did not escape the attention of the war-oriented Germans. All through the 30's, Von Braun and other German scientists diligently studied and experimented with liquid propelled rockets. Their efforts resulted in the deadly but inconclusive V-2. Thousands of these highly sophisticated (at that time) rockets were launched, and landed with often devastating results in England.

The Germans with their pre-eminence in rockets notwithstanding, were defeated by the Russians and Americans, who obtained as much material and as many men as they could carry away from German test and development sites.

This formed the nucleus of all subsequent rocket development activity in both countries. The major emphasis was on liquid propellants, despite its tempermental nature. One of the most severe problems, particularly for U.S. rockets, was combustion instability.

The phenomenon is a result of combustion at high flow rates. When hundreds of pounds of propellant are burned in a

Few people, other than employees, have ever visited the Propulsion Field Laboratory hidden in the Simi Hills above the San Fernando Valley.

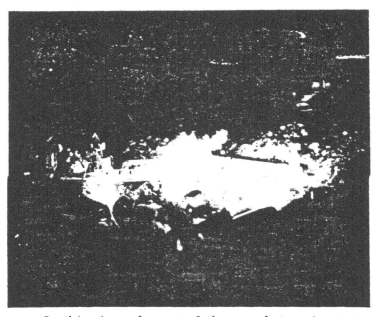

In this view of a set of three rocket engine test stands, we see the San Fernando Valley just beyond the hill crests. The majority of the population were unaware of exactly what was taking place at the Field Laboratory.

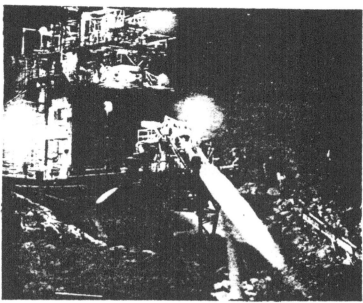

This test, VTS 2 at the Rocketdyne Propulsion Field Laboratory, was destroyed by a tremendous explosion in the 1950s. None of this information ever reached the American public. Disasters have always been squelched by NASA when possible.

A test of hypergolic propellants: nitrogen tetroxide and hydrazine (UDMH) at the Field Lab. Such tests were dangerous in the extreme due to the toxicity of the propellants in their burned or unburned state. The residents of the nearby San Fernando valley were not told of the nature or danger of this type of testing.

short time, strange effects take place. Acoustic transients present in this type of "continuous explosion" can trigger resonant conditions.

In other words, the high noise levels (as much as 150 db) cause anomalies in propellant burning. Standing waves possessing high kinetic content flash back and forth within the chamber. In microseconds, these waves can concentrate high temperatures at certain points within the rocket chamber, burning the thin walls through and causing total engine failure.

As a witness to many rocket engine tests at the Santa Susana lab, I saw many failures, blowups and premature engine cutoffs due to incipient disaster. Even after the relatively modest Atlas engine cluster was accepted by the Air Force for use in the Atlas ICBM, failures occurred with repeated regularity.

For example, on April 20, 1964, the DOD announced that the Air Force had 13 consecutive failures with Atlas D, E and F rockets in the summer and fall of 1963. This was at a time when the F-1, a much larger engine, was under intensive development. My point is this: if the Atlas couldn't achieve reliability after almost a decade of development, how could a far larger and more powerful rocket engine be successful? Further, the Atlas was a military missile engine, while the F-1 was intended to transport human beings.

As late as the spring of 1963, special contracts were awarded to Rocketdyne to try to determine the cause of failures, most of them believed to be based on combustion instability. Subsequently, little information ever reached the public concerning this problem. Was the problem solved? Was it partially solved? Answers to these questions will not be forthcoming until NASA makes these data available to the public.

A formerly secret picture of an Atlas rocket engine on a static test stand.

The famous Atlas engine operating at full power during a static (held down) test at the Rocketdyne Field Laboratory. Again, it is important to note that all personnel are safe within sturdy blockhouses or behind barriers far distant when this engine is functioning. There are good reasons for this safety procedure, all based on experience.

"I doubt if I could have flown my (Mercury and Gemini) missions if they had encountered as many foul-ups as the Apollo craft."

—Walter Shirra, February, 1966

4

Why Simulation

"If you can't make it, fake it."

—Old aerospace saying

Shortly after my assignment to the Rocketdyne Propulsion Field Laboratory in 1956, I made a most fascinating discovery: the lunchless picnic. It seems that there were many fine trysting places on the 1,880 rugged, rock-strewn acres that comprised the lab. These did not escape the attention of the young men and women who were free to roam this Western landscape, both off and on assignment.

For example, photo crews often took jeeps to high promontories to photograph rocket engine test stands in the process of construction. There was no objection to taking along a female companion if this did not conflict with work schedules. The nooks and crannies, the low-branched live oaks, the tall wild oats in the spring and people's natural proclivities to romance took care of the rest. Thus, the so-called lunchless picnic became an everyday reality at PFL, or Piffle, as it became known to the natives.

On occasion, these rendevous were documented with some negatives and positives processed, of course, in the photo lab during the graveyard shifts.

Personally, I found this relaxed, permissive atmosphere both amusing and contradictory. The latter, because, after all, in the spring of 1956 there was a pervading climate of doom: unless we could develop an engine to launch our hydrogen bombs over Russia first, the Russians would surely do us in at an earlier date. So frantic was the pace, that I was actually hired in on overtime, although my knowledge of rockets and technical writing both equalled zero.

To watch Bobby, the Area II photographer, and Betty, the still photo file clerk, go bounding off in an Air Force jeep without either lunch or Speed Graphic, was hard to compromise with the daily bulletins which reminded us of the missile gap. But I soon discovered that the need of the Air Force for a cluster of engines to propel the Atlas Inter-continental ballistic missile always or nearly always took the back seat to anything even remotely entertaining and immediate.

This attitude went far beyond giggly rolls in the tall weeds behind Vertical Test Stand II. Actually, anything personal always had a DX plus priority. (DX was the government's highest priority designation. With it, anything could be obtained . . . men, materials, money; and no one could offer a valid or viable protest). A few items recalled at random will make this point clear.

Item One: A leading engineer charged with an important aspect of rocket testing had a fine set of patio supports fabricated from the best quality stainless steel. Although they could have been purchased at any home improvement supply center for $2 each in plain steel, nothing was too good for this important leader of rocket engine development. I surveyed the handsome foursome and asked my friend how much he thought they cost the USAF and thus the taxpayers: "Oh, I'd say about $90 each, if you don't count the overhead."

Item Two: Of course, the tab for G-jobs, as personal work was always called, was not always this high. For example, if I wanted a photograph of my unit to show my children, this could be arranged for the asking.

Item Three: But then there was the stange case of Vernier Supply Group. An instance of scientific reality that certainly conflicted with the political goals of the pre-Apollo era. It seems that after the successful development of the small Vernier rocket engine for the Atlas engine cluster, the unit was transferred to the main plant in Canoga Park, some 25 minutes away by car or company bus.

Author(standing left) with crew of technical publications unit at Propulsion Field Laboratory (Rocketdyne, a division of North American Aviation) about 1961. Others are Les Helson (standing right), Norma Bachman (seated left) and Ginny Beery (seated right).

No one, however, thought to transfer the small group that had functioned as a logistical supply unit for the main Vernier group. Therefor, these people, unit leader, his secretary, a unit clerk and four purchasing agents -- seven in all -- remained behind at PFL with no activity to help pass the time. Rather than alert the main unit of their forlorn abandonment, the unit leader assumed the attitude that if they were called for, they would come. If not, they would jolly well stay at free-and-easy "Piffle" for all time!

And so the modern personification of Custer's Last Stand, the doughty Vernier Supply Group, remained on for almost six months. What did they do? Well, fortunately, Rocketdyne had a patented time save form known as the AVO (Avoid Verbal Orders). A simple piece of paper, it was used to make and receive various communications interdepartmentally. Thus, the unit leader merely dictated a variety of tasks to be performed within the unit in situ, and then saw that these tasks were promptly carried out.

Anyone who has spent any time at all in the armed forces, in civil service or any related bureaucratic activity, will instantly recognize the wisdom of this unit leader in "not making any waves". This latter phrase was a watchword throughout North American Aviation and meant exactly what it implies . . . as long as the paychecks are delivered on time and are reasonably correct, don't cause any uproar.

It is a tribute to the Rocketdyne Industrial Engineering Department's astuteness and diligence that no more than six months passed before this group was discovered hiding in the corner of Building Delta, Area II, and promptly transferred to Canoga Park. Why hadn't the parent group missed them? Oh, there's always lots to do without having to call on your supply group for entertainment . . .

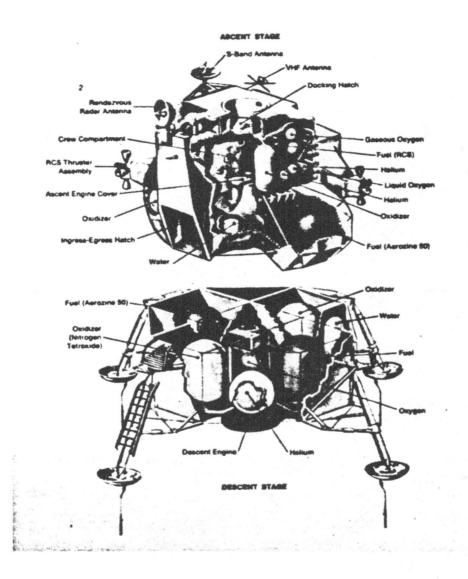

The complexity of the LEM is shown in this cutaway. Failure of an item (fuel tank, battery, igniter) could doom any mission, and most of the equipment was untried in space as of July, 1969.

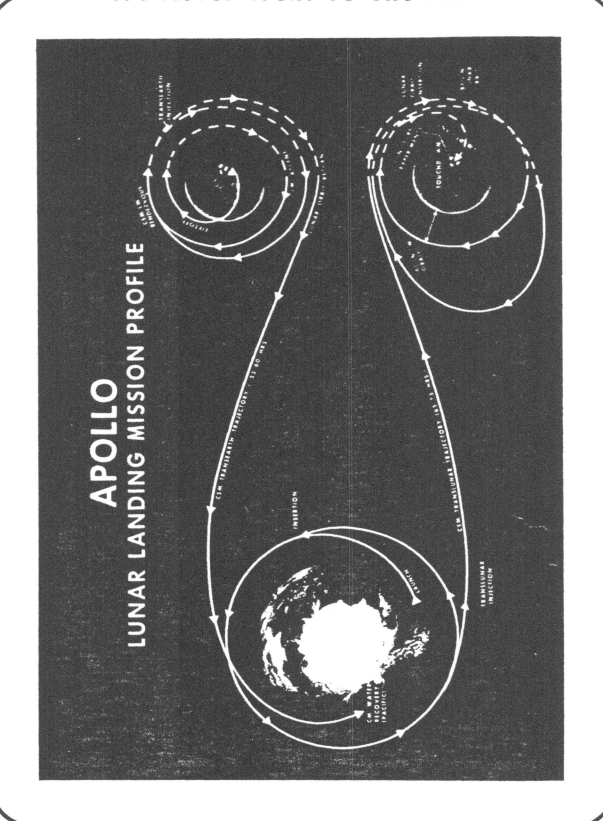

1. Lift-Off
2. S-IC Powered Flight
3. S-IC Engine Cutoff
4. S-IC/S-II Separation, S-IC Retro, S-II Ullage
5. S-II Engines Ignition
6. S-IC/S-II Interstage Jettison
7. Launch Escape Tower Jettison
8. S-II Powered Flight
9. S-II Engines Cutoff
10. S-II/S-IVB Separation, S-II Retro, S-IVB Ullage
11. S-IVB Engine Ignition
12. S-IVB Powered Flight
13. S-IVB Engine Cutoff
14. Earth Parking Orbit
15. Begin Systems Status Checks
16. Command Service Module (CSM) Guidance System Reference Alignment
17. Orient for Translunar Injection
18. S-IVB Ullage
19. S-IVB Engine Ignition
20. Translunar Injection
21. CSM Separation from Lunar Module (LM) Adapter
22. CSM 180° Turnabout
23. CSM Docking With LM/S-IVB
24. CSM/LM Separation From S-IVB
25. CSM Guidance System Reference Alignment
26. Orient Space Craft Attitude For Midcourse Correction
27. SM Engine Ignition
28. 1st Midcourse Correction Translunar
29. Systems Status Checks Eat and Sleep Periods Data Transmit Periods
30. CSM Guidance System Reference Alignment

31. Orient Space Craft Attitude for Midcourse Correction
32. Midcourse Correction, If Required
33. System Status Checks Eat and Sleep Period Data Transmit Period
34. CSM Guidance System Reference Alignment
35. Orient S/C Attitude for Midcourse Correction
36. Final Midcourse Correction Translunar
37. CSM Guidance System Reference Alignment
38. Orient Space Craft Attitude for Lunar Orbit Insertion
39. Lunar Orbit Insertion
40. Begin Lunar Orbit
41. CSM Guidance System Reference Alignment
41A. 1st 2 Lunar Orbits 69 x 195 M
41B. Circularization Burn Beginning of 3rd Orbit
42. System Status Check
43. Pilot Transfer to LM
44. LM Systems Activation and Checkout
45. CSM/LM Separation
46. Orient LM for Descent Orbit insertion
47. Descent Orbit Insertion
48. LM Guidance System Reference Alignment
49. LM Descent
50. Touch Down
51. LM System Checkout
52. Explore Surface, Set Up Experiments
53. LM Prelaunch Checkout

54. Rendezvous Radar Track CSM
55. Liftoff
56. LM Ascent
57. Concentric Sequence Initiation
57A. Plane Change Initiate
58. Constant Delta Height Maneuver
58A. Terminal Phase Initiation
59. Midcourse Correction
60. Rendezvous Maneuvers
61. CSM/LM Initial Docking
62. Transfer Crew and Equipment from LM to CSM
63. CSM/LM Separation and LM Jettison
64. Determine Transearth Injection Thrusting Parameters
65. Transearth Injection
66. Systems Status Check Eat and Sleep Period Data Transmit Period
67. Orient CSM Attitude for Midcourse Correction
68. 1st Midcourse Correction Transearth
69. System Status Check Eat and Sleep Periods Data Transmit Periods
70. CSM Guidance System Reference Alignment
71. Orient CSM for Midcourse Correction
72. Midcourse Correction If Required
73. System Status Checks Eat and Sleep Periods Data Transmit Periods
74. CSM Guidance System Reference Alignment
75. Orient CSM for Midcourse Correction

76. Final Midcourse Correction,
77. CSM Guidance System Reference Alignment
78. Orient CSM for Command Module/Service Module (CM/SM) Separation
79. CM/SM Separation
80. Orient CM for Reentry
81. 400,000 ft. Attitude Penetration
82. Communication Blackout Period
83. Jettison Forward Heat Shield and Deploy Drogue Chute
84. Deploy Main Chute
85. Splashdown

The preceding page's illustration of the Lunar Landing Mission is made up of 85 separate maneuvers listed here. Statisticians say that completing this mission six times without a single failure is beyond probability.

5

THE MOON HOAX!
- Photographic Proof -

In this chapter is a photographic review of the Apollo Simulation Program. If a picture is truly worth a thousand words, than this section would fill an encyclopedia. Here is shown that NASA has created the evidence for their conviction.

The photographs presented here are in 4 groups showing their major areas of discrepancy. All the photos share common discrepancies such as no stars and reflections or lighting from areas of No Light. Study each photo carefully for each is an exact reproduction of an original NASA photograph.

Group 1

No Crater Under
LEM's Rocket !

The photographs in this group are taken from different angles of the Lunar Module resting on the moon's surface. In each it is clearly evident that the surface is undisturbed under the LM's rocket engine.

As you will see in group 2's photographs, the moon's surface is such that physical evidence would have been seen under the LM's powerful engine.

We Never Went To The Moon

During the last forty feet or so of descent, the rocket-engine exhaust sent the dust of the moon flying. Not billows of dust; instead, the disturbed particles flew out at low angles and high velocity, like rays of light, with no atmosphere to buoy them or impede them. Armstrong later described it as "much like landing through light ground fog." The moment the engine shut off, however, the view out the window was completely clear again.

Armstrong's maneuver took him more than 1,000 feet beyond where the autopilot would have set him down, cost an extra 40 seconds, and left only about 2 percent of usable fuel—about 400 pounds—for the descent engine.

But it meant a safe landing, and a gentle one—so gentle that the two men hardly felt it. Armstrong says that their downward speed was probably no more than one foot a second. And the footpads of the eight-ton craft (it weighed only a sixth of that on the moon) settled just an inch or two into the surface.

Courtesy National Geographic

Besides the disturbance of dust mentioned, (which the photos do not show) a mathematical error arose.

If 2 percent of the usable fuel is 400 pounds then 100% is 20,000 pounds, or ten tons. The entire Lunar Module only weighed eight tons.

In the "National Geographic" excerpt, Armstrong is quoted saying how dusty the LM's rocket engine was making the surface while landing, yet the photos show nothing disturbed.

Even the artists conceptions of the LM's landing show a large amount of swirling dust and a crater after landing.

Group 2

What Happened To The Dust?

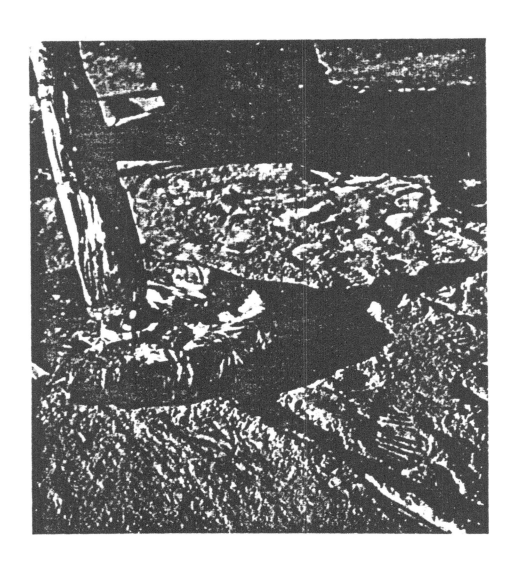

"*The exhaust dust was kicked up by the engine and this caused some concern in that it degraded our ability to determine not only our altitude and altitude-grade in the final phases, but also, and probably more importantly, our translational velocities over the ground.*"

— *ARMSTRONG*

In Armstrong's own words, enough dust was being disturbed to creat a hazard on landing. BUT WHERE IS THE DUST! As you can see in the 2 photographs of the LM's pads, not a spec of dust has settled on them.

Shown above is how easy dust and small rocks are disturbed with a light kick to the surface.

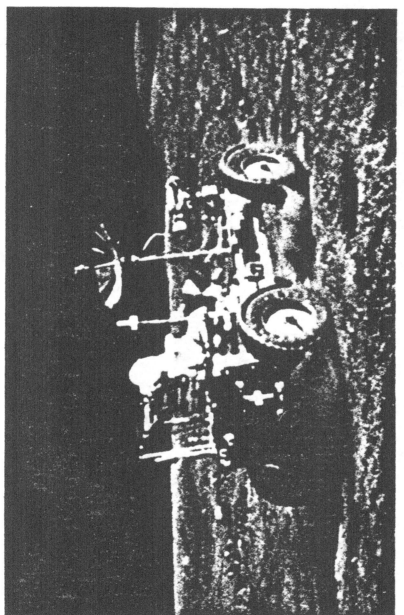

Here the Lunar Rover is throwing dust in all directions from its spinning tires. If dust is disturbed this easily, just think what a several thousand pound rocket thrust would do.

On the preceding page and above photos show how the dust seems to stick and accumlate on the wheels and fender of the Lunar Rover, but no dust stuck or even settled on the pads of the LM.

Also take notice of the two arrows placed on the photo on the preceding page. Notice how the small rocks and granular surface disappears suddenly into a smooth almost blurry surface. Could the background be nothing more than a large photograph and the foreground nothing more than gravel and dirt spread out on the floor of a large sound studio?

The surface of the moon was so soft and dusty that the astronaut's boot print sunk 1 to 2 inches deep into the surface.

Group 3

Reflections & Lighting?

In this group of photographs reflections are present on the face shields when they should be in the shadows.

On the preceding page Aldrin's face shield shows a vivid reflection of his shadow, the LM and Armstrong (cameraman) with no indication of artifical lighting. The sun is shining over his left shoulder — WHY THE REFLECTION.

In the photograph above the sun is directly behind the astronaut yet a bright reflection from his face shield.

The photos on the following page are different shots showing reflections where there should be shadows.

In addition to the reflection on the astronaut's face shield, there is excellent lighting on the stars and strips. With the sun to the left of the flag, it would appear to be impossible for this strong illumination to exist in the flag area.

Group 4

No Stars!

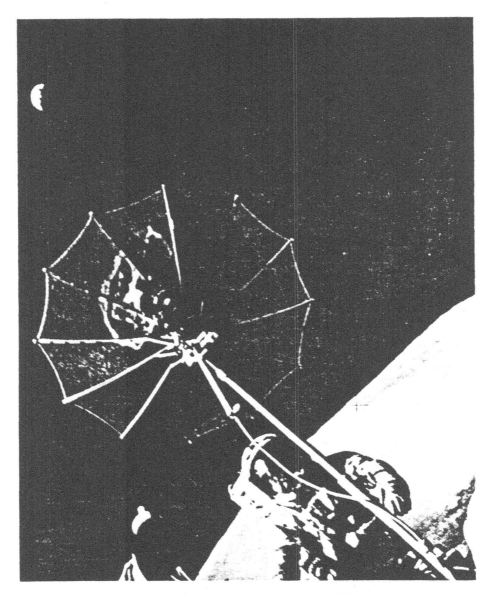

With no atmosphere on the moon to filter light from the heavens the stars would have shown with such brilliance that the sight would have been breathtaking. Why was no effort taken to photograph the stars or other planets? Not even in the background of the photographs that were shot was the presence of stars noted. WHY NO STARS? Could astronomers have picked apart a photo with man positioned and lighted stars?

We Never Went To The Moon

This photo of the moon was taken from Apollo 16, if it real wouldn't it be surrounded by stars?

6

Simulation
- How It Was Done -

"Site Y, as Los Alamos was called, was smaller than the other two secret cities of the Manhattan Project, Oak Ridge and Hanford. But, like them, its name did not appear on any map—neither was it used as an address."
—Stephen Groueff, "Manhattan Project, The Untold Story"

Once the decision to simulate all moon voyages was made, NASA and the Defense Intelligence Agency moved swiftly. A code name was created: ASP (Apollo Simulation Project), and the effort was divided into the following tasks:

1. Secret top level organization and management
2. Intensive security, including counter-intelligence
3. Undercover procurement of personnel
4. Clandestine equipment design, manufacture, installation and operation
5. Coverup communications, including wiretaps and taping
6. Covert planning and special projects (Aerospace "plumbers")

A detailed discussion of each of these tasks will best describe how the entire project was successfully conducted.

We Never Went To The Moon

Secret Top Level Organization And Management

"It was not easy (in 1943) to locate the Manhattan District. No such organization was listed in the phone book; no one seemed to know anything about it."

—Stephen Groueff

Since WWII, it has not been unusual for the United States to create special groups for clandestine political tasks. All are descended from the Office of Strategic Services (OSS), the brainchild of William J. Donovan. He convinced Roosevelt in 1942 that the U.S. needed a special organization to conduct secret intelligence activities, engage in special operations, wage psychological warfare and use any means to undermine the enemy's morale and interests.

One of the most sophisticated activities of OSS was research on subjects of strategic interest. In this effort they drew upon such high-level organization as the Office of Scientific Research and Development headed at one time by Vannevar Bush. Bush was a leading scientist associated with the Manhattan District.

Although the OSS was disbanded after the war, personnel of three of its branches were kept on duty and incorporated into the new Federal intelligence structure. On January 22, 1946, President Truman issued an executive letter establishing the Central Intelligence Agency (CIA).

Subsequently, the National Security Act of 1947 authorized the President to use the CIA to "perform such services of common concern as the National Security Council determines can be more efficiently accomplished centrally; to perform such other duties affecting the national security as the Council may from time to time direct."

It is not required that one be a constitutional lawyer to recognize the tremendous power these clauses give the President to use the CIA for covert political warfare.

The phrases "services of common concern" and "such other duties affecting the national security" have been interpreted as legal authority for such diverse activities as: the U-2

Author's conception of the ASP control center near Mercury, NV. Here, the top DIA simulation controllers directed the entire worldwide operaiton. Note maps of the then—AEC base on the wall and TV monitors of the moon "set".

episode, the Bay of Pigs invasion, the Pueblo, Tonkin Gulf, My Lai and Watergate.

These cancerous outgrowths of the original intent of the National Security Act reveal that the CIA became the American Gestapo as well as a close copy of the dreaded Russian OGPU. As such, they are more than capable of implementing and executing any covert effort. The ultimate implication is that the public is the enemy—to be manipulated, fooled and defrauded without mercy or conscience.

We Never Went To The Moon

The ASP Group

In 1961, the overall direction of ASP was coordinated under the aegis of a new federal entity, the Defense Intelligence Agency (DIA). As cited by L.B. Kirkpatrick in the book "The U.S. Intelligence Community", the DIA was "conceived as an organization to assist in the coordination of the military contributions of the nation."

Obviously the DIA was expertly contrived to "help" NASA with their technical problems by establishing a totally simulated moon mission. After all, as most aerospace insiders know, the Apollo project was actually a military mission to determine the feasibility of using the moon as a military base of operations against foreign powers. Furthermore, almost 75 per cent of all NASA effort was basically military—not space!

When the capability of controlling orbiting H-bombs became a reality, the moon became far less important to the Pentagon's planners. Who needs a moon base when it's possible to destroy any or all of the planet with bombs disguised as communications satellites that orbit the earth 24 hours a day, they reasoned.

However, despite this diminishment of interest, the military was still strongly supportive of any activity that would enhance U.S. prestige worldwide. Thus, the DIA was structured to provide services to NASA, as shown in the chart. How these various departments or divisions functioned is described in the interpretive tabulation.

Defense Intelligence School

Training center for ASP personnel: Washington and Nevada.

As could be suspected and anticipated through experience, this group was not only a managerial body but an action force that instigated, implemented and fulfilled the ASP project. Its budget was enormous but still less than the above ground Apollo effort; estimates range from four to seven billion dollars, as against more than 30 billion for the visible Apollo. Secrecy is expensive but, inversely, large sums often attract attention that can prove damaging to a covert operation.

In general, the ASP program was approached in the same manner as the production of the atomic bomb: total secrecy, total compliance and costs be damned! There was no margin for error. The prestige of the U.S. was at stake. Also, the national and international repercussions that would have resulted from exposure of the fraud would have dwarfed the Bay of Pigs or Watergate affairs.

Intensive Security Including Counter-Intelligence

"Not more than a half-dozen men were entrusted with complete information concerning the project and its objective, although a total of 800 were involved. Each floor of the building had an armed guard on duty. Burglar alarms were installed on all doors and windows. Everyone had two waste-baskets—one painted red for classified information. Every evening these were taken downstairs and their contents incinerated in the presence of a security officer. Only American citizens were permitted to work on the project and then only after being cleared by Intelligence Services. Visitors had to fill out a slip and tear off a stub of this slip. By so doing, they left, without suspecting it, their fingerprints on the specially sensitized paper of the stub . . . The word 'uranium' was never used."

—From "The Manhattan Project"

Although more than 300,000 persons were directly involved in the building of the atomic bomb (1942-45), no significant information whatsoever reached the public. Thus was established a viable precedent for ASP. The ASP managers could not only point to the Manhattan's success in secrecy, but could use their methods. After all, in an America which has been sliding towards a police state for years (wiretaps, no-knock, civilian surveillance), it was a relatively simple matter to apply these techniques of cloak and dagger to ASP.

Rigidly tight security develops itself a perfect position. Anyone can be excluded by the principle of "need to know". Since NASA has always been 75 per cent military and certainly ASP was in this catagory, preventing anyone high or low from seeing certain hardware, data or locations, was as easy as dropping a thick curtain. Further, anyone who comprised a threat or knew too much could be taken care of in a number of interesting ways. And all of these measures were justified as being the protection of the national interests.

One of the first security measures undertaken by the ASP Security Staff was the establishment of a base of operations.

Privacy With Recreational Opportunities

The chart which compares methods of connection with protection was used to determine the optimum location for the ASP base. Beyond these prosaic considerations was the exciting appeal of a nearby resort city. Thus, it was no accident that the ASP base was located 32 miles east of Mercury, Nevada. The land surrounding the base has long been controlled by the U.S. Air Force and the Atomic Energy Commission —a double threat to any interlopers.

In this view of the region it may be seen that any trespassers would show up instantly on the screens of the constantly-on TV monitors. Also, control of personnel through the few checkpoints could be accomplished with efficiency and dispatch.

The Mercury ASP base was desirable from a number of security-related standpoints:

1. Strange shipments could be delivered inside trucks marked with the dreaded "radiation" sign.
2. Staff could come and go via the heavily guarded airfield. An elaborate warning-wave-off radioradar protection system prevented any private planes from using the field except for dire emergencies. Even then, strangers were prevented from actually seeing anything of a compromising nature.
3. Odd noises, weird devices, excavations were permissible since no outsiders had visual or audio access.

Although termed Area 6 by the Atomic Energy Commission, this could be the headquarters of ASP near Mercury, NV. Note especially the air strips on the dry lake beyond the facility.

---

4. Coded communications could be made by regular or incredibly high frequency microwave radio.
5. Tensions could be relieved by making the less-than-one-hour trip to Las Vegas, a 24-hour-a-day, seven-days-a-week, anything-goes resort boasting more than 30 large casinos.

Last but far from least, a liason was established with the hidden rulers of Las Vegas, the crime organization chieftains. When needed, services could be exchanged on a mutually

We Never Went To The Moon

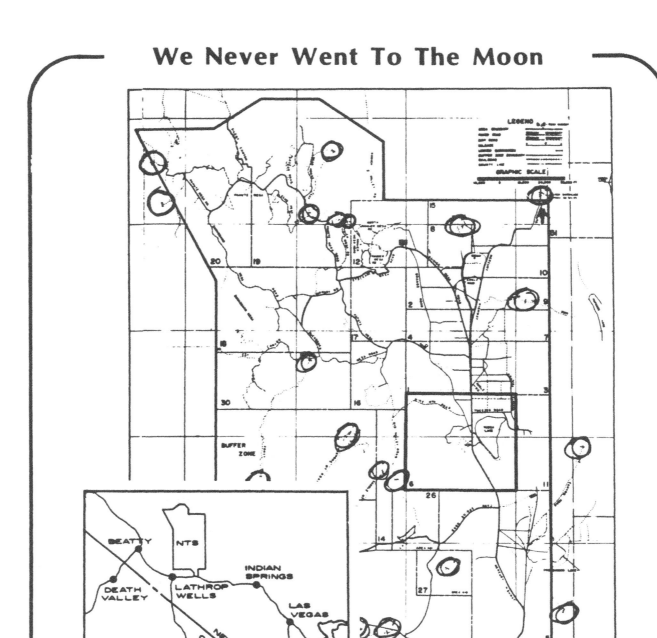

NEVADA TEST SITE = TOTAL SECURITY
Locked and guarded barricades are circled to show the
extent of control over the entire base of operations. The
area with the heavy line around it is location of photo from
previous page (Area 6). Arrow in lower right shows location
of Mercury, NV. Inset in lower left shows NTS's isolation
which is much needed for total security.

Almost as secret as Los Alamos was during WW II, Mercury, NV is virtually unknown to most Americans. What deep secrets does this small city hold?

Another secret installation probably related to the ASP effort. Isolation has always been the key to such activities whether a concentration camp or a secret rocket base. Who could enter here unseen?

More importantly, note the striking resemblance of the terrain to a lunar landscape!

beneficial basis, i.e., large sums of money for use of expert "button men". The Cosa Nostra staff presented no problems for ASP Security; they had centuries of practice in remaining silent.

> NOTE: U.S.-Mafia criminal cooperation was hardly new. During the invasion of Sicily during WWII, Mafia chieftains aided American troops.

Undercover Procurement Of Personnel

Staffing ASP was not as difficult as it might appear to the layman. First, everyone has a price although sometimes the price is one's life. Notwithstanding diehards, recruiting of ASP people went swingingly. People love to know secrets and they also love to have lots of money to spend. ASP provided both.

Salaries of $50,000 for minor technicians were not uncommon. We have deleted the pay of higher staff personnel out of sympathy for the taxpayer who might be reading this chapter. In addition to salaries, expense accounts for "rest and relaxation" were virtually unlimited. It is interesting to note that during the build-up of ASP facilities near Mercury, income for many of the Las Vegas casinos hit new highs.

Three major categories of ASP personnel existed:

1. Top level management, including DIA and supplemental agency support.
2. Interface personnel, many on "need to know" basis.
3. The astronauts themselves.

Recruiting of the first two categories was done on a money first, patriotism second, basis. It was eminently successful. More descretion was required in obtaining the cooperation of astronauts. For these dedicated and brave men, the following arguments were used:

A. The moon mission was tremendously important to the continuance of the United States as a (or THE) power in political, military, scientific and technical areas.

B. Billions of dollars and several lives had been spent so far; to scratch the mission at this point (1963) would be disastrous to the administration from a public relations standpoint. NASA was in the same position as a Vegas gambler who is in too deep to quit. (NASA's self-interest was also a strong influence: it is a truism that all bureaucracies seek to expand or at least perpetuate themselves.)

C. There would be no danger since the men would not exit the earth's gravitational field.

D. Fame and fortune would be theirs, tarnished only slightly by the fact that the voyage would be illusionary.

E. Intimations that refusal could bring reprisals ranging from demotion to in-flight "accidents". There was no need to remind the candidates of the eight astronauts who had died accidently during the early phases of Apollo.

NOTE: Thomas R. Baron, an employee of North American Aviation, Apollo's prime contractor, submitted a 500 page report on the inadequacies of the program following the fatal fire on Pad 34. Shortly thereafter, Baron was killed when his car apparently stalled in front of a locomotive.

In addition to these cogent persuasions, the men approached had lifetime histories of obedience. All were or had been in the armed forces and were accustomed to accepting assignments regardless of risk or rather, in spite of risk.

Most pilots are extroverted, game-playing individuals. Thus, it was a relatively simple matter to train the astronauts to play their respective roles in the high drama of ASP. As with most machinery, strains may develop in humans under stress. The recent breakdown of Edwin A. Aldrin, the lunar module pilot, could be an indication of second thoughts.

In summary, ASP recruitment was an unqualified success. That no information has been revealed to this day is not surprising. A CIA-sponsored group known as Air America is noted for its two distinct types of alumni: The silent and the silenced.

We Never Went To The Moon

Clandestine Equipment Design, Manufacture
Installation And Operation: Simulation Hardware And
Secret Base

Once a base was established and security in effect, the preparation of simulation equipment could begin.

A complete set of the moon was built in an underground cavern at the ASP base. Every location that would be used for landings was created in exact detail. This elaborate sound stage was code named Copernicus, after one of the lunar craters. It soon earned the name "Cuss" because of problems in lighting and sound.

In addition, scale models of the earth, sun, moon and other bodies were carefully built and mounted within a planetarium-like device so that they could be positioned and photographed with accuracy, repeatability and believability.

The underground sound stage resembled those at a major Hollywood studio complete with overhead catwalks for lighting, camera dolly tracks and other basic filming and TV equipment. In addition, there was a plethora of special effects tools, including high intensity lighting to imitate the harsh glare of sunlight on the airless moonscape.

All scenes of the Lunar Excursion Module (LEM) were filmed on this set with the astronauts as "stars". There were no more problems than would appear during the filming of "Star Trek", "2001, A Space Odyssey", or "Silent Running". After all, Hollywood grips and gaffers, cameramen and directors had acquired long experience in science fiction film production. A plus for the project was the advantage of filming silent. All voices and equipment sounds were dubbed in by an elaborate sound creation and dubbing studio immediately adjacent to the moon set.

SPECIAL NOTE: In the film "Diamonds Are Forever", with Sean Connery playing the role of Agent 007 - James Bond, there is a curious and unexplained scene. He enters a secret research facility in the Nevada desert by ruse. Suddenly he finds himself in a large room in which there is an authentic moon landscape. Lumbering about in their clumsy space suits are two would-be astronauts. Nothing happens, the scene is not explained, and the viewer is left to ponder its significance. Could it be . . .? Yes, it could!

Also installed at the "Cuss" base was the master control of which the so-called Mission Control and the Spacecraft Center at Houston were merely satellites or slaves. The master control of Cuss (MASCONCULL) collected all data, programmed it into a computer which then coordinated the entire moon landing simulation. Since all releases were by well-edited tape, there was no chance of a blooper. Again, the total control of news by the American corporate state set an effective precedent for the totally controlled output of MASCONCULL. From prelaunch countdown to the final descent to the ocean, all sound and video transmissions emanated from the flawless and mechanistic heart of a specially modified IBM 370-C computer.

Simulation Propulsion Hardware

The term "hardware" became a standard term in the aerospace industry for anything that was not stored in a file cabinet or recorded on tape. In short, it meant anything that was manufactured: from an Automatically controlled solenoid to an IDIOT (Intermediate Digital On-Line Transducer).

From the date of the decision to simulate, a modified hardware program was conducted. For example, the Saturn C-5 moon rocket assembly was built to specifications with one major modification: instead of the totally unreliable F-1 engines, five booster engines of the more dependable B-1 type as used in the C-1 cluster for the Atlas missile were used.

Although a cluster of five B-1 engines produced only one-half of the output of a single F-1 chamber, the power (750,000 pounds thrust) was sufficient to launch the virtually empty Apollo vehicle. If the rocket had been in its designed form it would have weighed 6,000,000 pounds, or 3,000 tons fully loaded. This is the weight of a U.S. naval destroyer, further pointing out the total impracticality of the venture. However, by eliminating every aspect of the moon voyage—fuel, heavy engines, LEM vehicles, etc., the total weight of the modified shortrange, simulated voyage Apollo was less than one-twentieth of the original, or about 150 tons. This loading was well within the capabilities of the B-1 propulsion units. Also, since the originally planned two million parts were reduced to a mere 150,000 gadgets, the success of the limited mission was virtually assured.

However, even C-1 Atlas engines were known to explode on the pad or shortly following launch. Thus, the escape module for the astronauts was left intact and functioning. If there had been an accidental loss of thrust or other mishap, it would have been simple to have the "saved" astronauts emerge from the escape module after its recovery.

Coverup Communications, Including Wiretaps And Taping

Although the most critical element from the standpoint of press and public relations interface, simulated communications and printed data were technically the simplest to produce.

First, an agreement was obtained by DIA and ASP representatives working with and through the semisecret Council on Foreign Relations. This agreement being a reciprocal one that would ensure silence on any revelatory Apollo information by major foreign powers.

Russia was the only nation that had the sophisticated tracking radar capable of following Apollo and thus sabotaging the simulation. But Russia was planning extensive commercial exchange with the U.S. and intelligently recognized that they would gain no real advantage by destroying the U.S. myth. After all, their space program had always been ahead of ours and this fact was well-established worldwide.

Actually, there has never been a real problem between or among major nations where control of the masses has been a consideration, i.e., cold and hot wars to keep the masses occupied while they are being fleeced before slaughter. For further information in this area, read "The Rich And The Super-Rich" by Phillip Lundborg.

We Never Went To The Moon

The presentation of "on-scene" data was divided into these categories:

1. Visual presentations to the public or uncleared personal.
   A. Launch
   B. Re-entry (although out of sight of carrier crews)
2. Radio transmissions during launch, trip to moon, exploration and return.
3. TV transmission from the moon.
4. Still pictures; black and white and color.

Visual Presentations

Hair-raising for the simulators but most convincing to the public were the launches. After all, if people could drive to the Cape, park and see an immense rocket lift itself off the pad, was this not the ultimate proof that a trip was, indeed, being made to the moon itself? The fact that once out of sight, the vehicle traveled a sub-orbital trajectory to the south polar sea (and jettisoned), did not diminish in any way the blazing glory of the launch to the moon.

The return to the earth by the astronauts in their re-entry module was far less risky than the launch. This was true since it was effected by dropping the module from a C-5A cargo plane. Just prior to this drop, they were picked up at a super-secret, well camouflaged island south of Hawaii.

It is interesting to note that the module was always out of the carrier's crew. Had the simulators desired, it would have been possible to drop the module into the Pacific from a far-ranging nuclear submarine. However, the plan method was chosen since it required a smaller crew "in the know" and ease of security that evolves from a hidden air base (Taura-moto Archipelago.)

Radio Transmissions

Of utmost simplicity, once installed and checked out, was the radio data transmitted "from" the moon vehicle. Secret, leased, and well-secured telephone lines were connected to the antennae inputs of all space communications centers. These included the major tracking stations in Australia, Africa, and the West Coast of the United States.

To accomodate amateur radio operators who might want to tune into it, identical broadcasts were made from an orbiting satellite. So perfect were all of these simulations, that the momentary blackout when the module was supposed to be behind the moon was faithfully reproduced.

Television Broadcasts

Unquestionably, the most interesting and entertaining for all concerned (simulators and fools alike) were the scenes of astronauts gamboling about the lunar set. In addition, these delightful frolics were really elementary exercises for the stage crews. After all, decades of special-effects development for the motion picture industry preceded the need for this expertise.

A curious anomaly occurred with respect to this phase of the simulation. The set had to be photographed through filters and electronic "noise" had to be added to avoid a too-perfect picture. Otherwise, these scenes would resemble too closely the action from "Star Trek" and other science fiction presentations. Even so, many viewers in bars and country clubs all over the U.S. suspected rather loudly that the scenes were fake; little of this reached the newspapers.

Note that in the montage of photographs of the astronauts "at work" on the moon that the simulation was a lesson in simplicity itself. With a totally black "space" background, and a rough, but firm, moon surface and LEM featured prominently, the reasonably authentic lunar scene was well within the capabilities of motion picture set designers and special-effects experts. Range marks (in the form of an "X" or cross) were added, providing an uncanny resemblance to reality - a tribute to the painstaking work of the simulators on an unlimited budget.

The photographs of moon models created by NASA, early

in the Apollo program, show how simple it was to take authentic looking shots of the moon in space. The simulators had a choice of several expensive Earth models for their "blue-green island in space" photos. Again, highly developed Hollywood techniques allowed many types of pictures to lie to us with great believability. When typical NASA press shots are compared with Hollywood stills for comparison, it is easy for the public to see what I am talking about.

Planning And Special Projects

This department was charged with the overall responsibility for planning and direction of the simulation. They also undertook to cover up any errors of theirs or any other ASP group.

Using the proven principles of the PERT system (a U.S. Navy method for coordinating many different activities simultaneously), this group generated a flexible but effective plan of action.

Favorable Publicity Released Through All Media

The astronauts and their families were depicted in a syrupy, sugar-coated fashion. The media coverage of various flights and tests, and their relative success, and the overall advantages of space flight in general, were heavily slanted in favor of NASA. Many articles were ghostwritten for such characters as James E. Webb and Wernher von Braun, and were given favorable placement in popular science magazines, along with diagrams of supposed space trips, photographs of lunar landing vehicles, space suits, and space food and drink, including a new drink called Tang.

Summary

PASP was a most important arm of ASP. They insured that few if any questions would be asked. If questioners persisted, they found themselves deluged with offers they couldn't refuse. The limited number of recalcitrants found it hard to swim with formfitting cement tennis shoes . . .

NOTE: A complete schedule and chronology of the simulated moon flight is presented. Another example of the work of the PASP Group.

Schedule and Chronology of Simulated Moon Flights

ITEM	REMARKS
L-72 hours, pre launch activities	Normal with the exception of substituted flight hardware. Example: B-1 booster placed within F-1 combustion chambers. LoxRP-1 combo rather than touted LH 2 O2.
L-1 hour, highly publicized and photographed entry of the astronauts into the Apollo vehicle	Analogous to a magician putting his "victim" into the box preparatory to sawing him in half.
L-20 minutes	The three astronauts depart the module via a high speed elevator. They go to heavily secured room in which there is an exact duplicate of the flying module. During this transitional period the TV picture is "lost accidentally."

Launch + one second

Normal in appearance with the five B-1 boosters functioning as F-1's.

L + 23 minutes

Following booster engine cutoff (BECO) a mock J-2 second stage cuts in. This is followed by a third stage mock J-2 which places the Apollo into a parking orbit. Meanwhile, the astronauts are flown to the moon set in Nevada by high altitude jet. Communication switchover to Nevada takes place.

Inputs of a phantom Apollo vehicle are now transmitted to the Deep Space Instrumentation Facilities at Goldston, Calif.; Johannesburg, South Africa; and Woomera, Australia.

L + 2 hours

All ASP systems are "GO". The Apollo has been jettisoned into the South Polar Sea. The three astronauts are comfortably seated in their subterranean module mockup surrounded by top ASP directors. Within this fantastic and well-equipped building is ever conceivable luxury, including a few of the shapliest showgirls from

Las Vegas, cleared for secret, of course.

Other than an occasional check with Mission Control in Houston, the astronauts are free to wander about and play the slots, sample the 24-hour buffet from the Dunes and watch color TV broadcasts from a private Telstar satellite.

NOTE: It has been alleged that one of the astronauts socked an ASP official in a dispute over a showgirl named Peachy Keen, but this has not been authenticated by our source of information.

L + 72 hours

Activities of the astronauts pick up as lunar holding orbit is approached. Moon set held in readiness for "touch-down". Studio grips and gaffers sprinkle moon dust on moon rocks, adjust lighting from sun arc. Green cheese sandwiches are served.(?)

L + 74 hours

The astronauts assume their respective positions. The lunar orbiting pilot remains behind in the command module while the "landing party" enters the LEM for the trip to the moon's surface.

(SOUNDS OF ENGINES STARTING, METAL CLANKING WITH VOICE OVER):

ARMSTRONG: "Is my antenna out? OK, now we're ready to hook up the LEC here."

ALDRIN: "Now that should go down . . . (static) . . . put the bag up this way. That's even. Neil, are you hooked up to it?"

ARMSTRONG: "Yes, OK, now we need to hook this?"

With all TV cameramen in position, the director calls for "lights, camera, action". Protected by a seven second delay in transmission and the watchful eye of the ASP moon walk director, the exciting scenes of the moon landing take place. The commander makes his well-rehearsed remark as he steps carefully from the LEM to the meticulously prepared surface of "moon", just 90 miles north of the bright lights and jangling slot machines of Las Vegas. NOTE: It's not a great performance, but good enough considering the actors and the audience.

The balance of the flight is almost an anti-climax. The return to the LEM, the reunion with the orbiting command module, the routine trip back to earth and touchdown. Simulated re-entry involves a minimum of equipment: simply a command module dropped from a C-5A. The astronauts are flown to a small atoll south of Hawaii; they board the plane, enter the module and are dropped safely just out of sight of the pickup carrier.

LANDING PLUS 21 DAYS

A team of ASP psychologists determines that the astronauts require a transitional period before confronting the press directly. This is necessary to:

1. Eliminate guilt feelings
2. Study and memorize moon data.
3. Practice responding to questions.

In short, orient themselves so that they behave like returning heroes instead of highly paid actors.

LANDING PLUS 22 DAYS

On their own but closely watched, the astronauts do their utmost to exude the aura of triumph, the facade of victory. For the majority of viewers, the simulation is a success.

Reprise

The schedule is exact but flexible; flexibility lends authenticity. In all, a difficult operation, but far less so than a genuine trip to the moon would have been.

7

Visual Aspect
Of Simulation

THE RELATIONSHIP BETWEEN THE FILM "2001" AND THE APOLLO PROJECT

Ever since German soldiers were shown spearing babies on their bayonets in WWI propaganda films, the motion picture industry has been a tool of the corporate state to capture human minds. During WWII, for example, I recall a steady stream of films glorifying war and portraying the Japanese people as slant-eyed devils. Movies have been used to push cigarettes (Bogart was their top salesman), fast cars and women's fashions.

It is my contention that Stan Kubrick's film, "2001, A Space Odyssey" was made for three reasons:
1. The usual one . . . profit.
2. With government sponsorship, to sell the concept of space travel prior to the Apollo missions.
3. To provide the technical know-how for creating all Apollo stills and motion pictures ON EARTH!

As Stan himself says,

"The screen is a magic medium. It has such power that it can retain interest as it conveys emotions and moods that no other art form can hope to tackle."

Faking the Apollo flights was a demonstration of filmic magic as we shall see. But first let's examine the time table. Mae Brussell, one of the world's leading conspiracy investigators, stresses the importance of examining the time framework of a suspected hoax.

1962   Increasing reliability problems with liquid propellant rocket engines, particularly hypergolics.

1963   AF interest in solid propellants causes phase-out of liquid propelled ICBM's.

1964   Scientific community expresses increasing doubt as to feasibility of manned lunar landings.

1965   Production begins on "2001" in London with NASA indoctrinated advisors (Frederick Ordway for example)

1968   Film premiered in L.A.

As everyone knows, the following year astronauts allegedly landed on the moon.

Thus, the time sequence is perfect. Americans were conditioned by "2001" to expect to see a certain quality in space films. But also, to come to expect that "reality" would be slightly different than the fantasy shown on the local theater screen. By cleverly blurring the line between fact and fantasy, a degree of confused acceptance evolves.

This is quite similar to that which exists in many other areas of public concern and interest. For example, we are led to believe that our food supply is guaranteed pure by the FDA. But that tool of the food industry allows more than 5,000 additives to be incorporated into our daily bread, meat and vegetables. And the graph showing increasing use of food additives exactly matches that showing increasing cancer in the U.S. While the AMA and the Department of Health, Education and Welfare assure us that we have the best medical care in the world, U.S. male longevity ranks 37th among the world's nations. The Social Security Administration has promised everyone a check upon reaching 65 but investigations have proven that the SS funds are non-existent and that the government itself is six trillion dollars in the hole!

Fortunately, people are becoming increasingly aware of government lies and deceit since, as Lincoln said, you cannot fool all of the people all the time. When food tastes odd, gives us cancer and when SS checks buy little or nothing, we simply must revalue government data. The same holds true for Apollo. So let's take a look at some photographic evidence. Compare views provided by NASA with those produced by the special effects team from the film "2001."

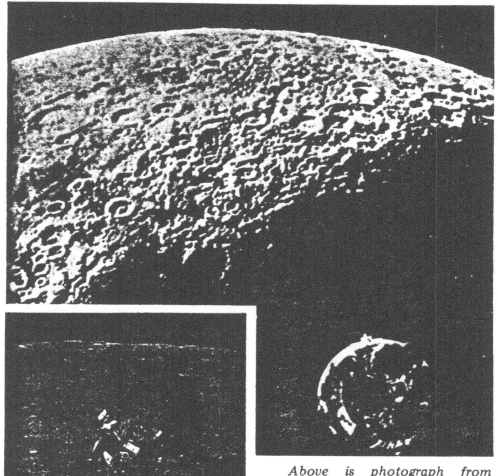

Above is photograph from "2001". Moon is transparency of telescopic picture of real Moon, re-photographed on animation stand.

Moon-shuttle Aries is a still photograph of model two feet in diameter shot on horizontal camera in order to get the longest track movement as it moves away. Movement of Aries was made by visualizing its relative movement against background and translating it simply to a first-and-last frame position.

Is the inset photo, to the left, the real LEM or a photograph of a 2 foot model over a Moon transparency?

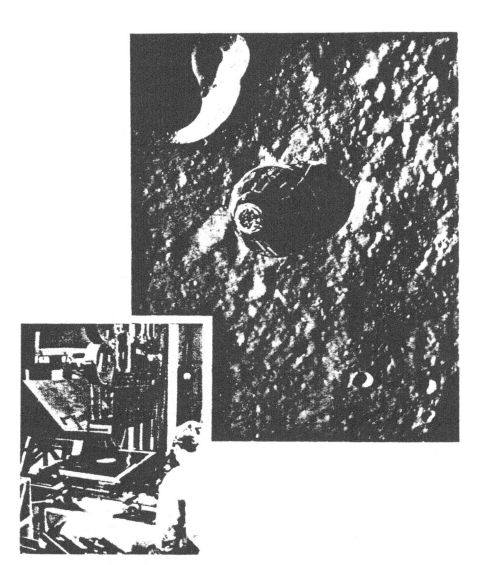

Above is an Apollo Command Module orbiting the Moon. Smaller photo to the left shows how "2001" simulated this same type shot, using an 8X10 moon plate being photographed on a 65mm Oxberry animation stand.

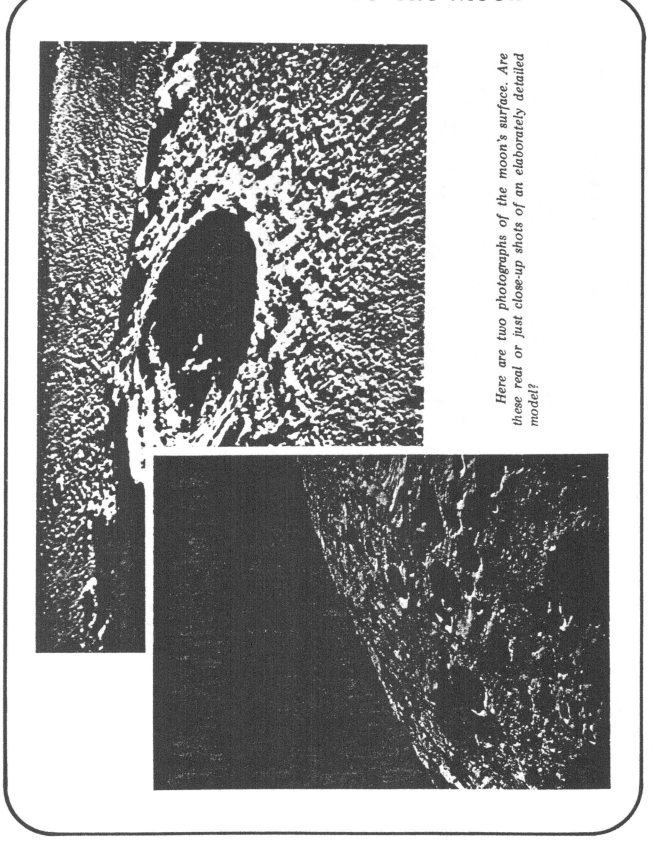

Here are two photographs of the moon's surface. Are these real or just close-up shots of an elaborately detailed model?

SPACE HOAXES ARE NOTHING NEW!

Space walks can be faked. Lloyd Mallan, who wrote a series of articles on Russian space hoaxes, proved beyond a reasonable doubt that it was possible to simulate extravehicular activity. Science and Mechanics published Mallan's material in 1966 in a special issue shown here. With sufficient reader interest, it may be possible to reproduce this issue for distribution.

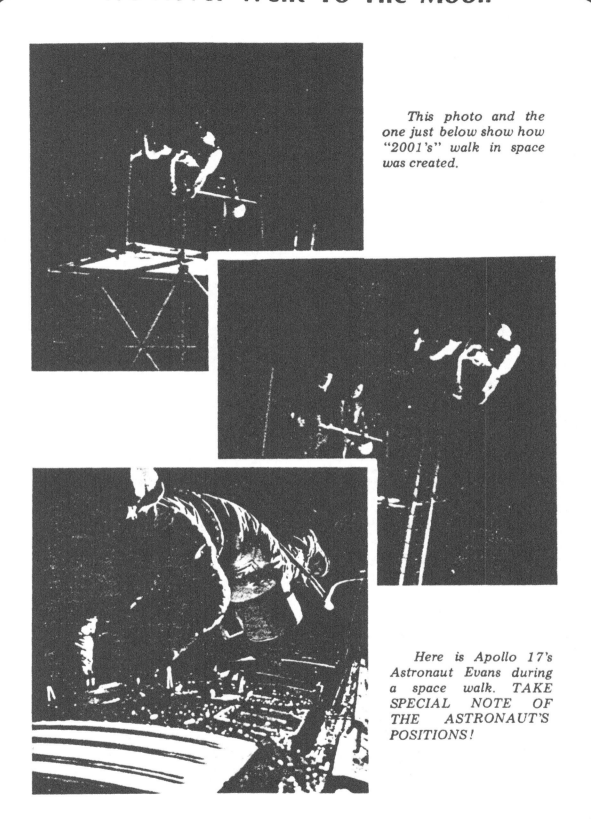

This photo and the one just below show how "2001's" walk in space was created.

Here is Apollo 17's Astronaut Evans during a space walk. TAKE SPECIAL NOTE OF THE ASTRONAUT'S POSITIONS!

We Never Went To The Moon

Did Kubrick (read NASA) have any assistance in preparing these stills and films? You can bet you last inflated Federal Reserve Note he did. Here's just a few of the above-ground organizations, agencies, people and other entities that provided everything needed AT NO COST!

Aerojet-General Corporation
Covina, California
   Instrumentation design and rationale, particularly for vehicle monitoring and display.

Aeronautical Chart and Information Center
St. Louis, Missouri, and Washington branch: Arlington, Virginia
   Charts of vast areas of the lunar surface, detailed data on Pic de Midi lunar photography, and support in obtaining such photography. Also, charts of the surface of Mars. In Washington: photographs of Earth taken from high-altitude rockets and from satellites.

Aerospace Medical Division
Wright-Patterson Air Force Base, Ohio
   Full pressure spacesuit design, operating instructions, use and accessories.

USAF School of Aerospace Medicine
San Antonio, Texas
   Photography of the Earth seen from extreme altitude manned balloons (Manhigh). Obtention of medical data in support of space medical aspects of film.

Department of the Air Force
The Pentagon, Washington, D. C.
   Nuclear rocket propulsion

Air Force Cambridge Research Laboratories
Bedford, Massachusetts
   Extreme altitude photography.

Analytical Laboratories, Ltd.
Corsham, Wiltshire, England
   Biological and medical instrumentation for centrifuge and for research panels for planetary and planetary moon probing.

Army Map Service
Washington, D. C.
   Maps of the moon.

U. S. Army Natick Laboratories
Natick, Massachusetts
   Data and photographs of space foods and associated equipment.

Barnes Engineering Co.
Stamford, Connecticut
   Design concepts of telescopes and antennas, and their console instrumentation.

Bell Telephone Laboratories, Inc.
Murray Hill, New Jersey
   1. Space Station V's picture- or vision-phone design, including rationale of routines to be followed in conducting orbit-Earth communications on a regular commercial basis. Assistance included typical jargon to be employed.
   2. Communications console for Discovery's centrifuge, including design and means of routine and nonroutine transmitting and receiving. Typical jargon was suggested.

Bendix Field Engineering Corp.
Owings Mills, Maryland
   Control centers, consoles, and readout devices of manned space flight network.

Boeing Company, Aero-Space Division
Seattle, Washington
   Space simulation facilities information and photographs.

Chrysler Corp.
New Orleans, Louisiana
   Interplanetary missions of scientific nature, particularly use of spaceship-mounted telescopes.

Computer Control Co.
Framingham, Massachusetts
   Computer operations, terminology, console jargon.

Department of Defense
Washington, D. C.
   Color photography of Earth and general support in obtaining information of DoD space activities.

Douglas Aircraft Co.
Santa Monica, California
   Instrumentation; vehicle design; console layouts; space vehicle films.

Detailed documentation on experiments that could be made from Discovery of the asteroids and the planet Jupiter, and its twelve moons.

Jet Propulsion Laboratory, California Institute of Technology
Pasadena, California
Spacecraft information, photography of lunar surface mission, analysis of the asteroid belt and Jupiter fly-by probes.

Langley Research Center
Hampton, Virginia
Detailed photographic tour of the center; gathering of large quantities of technical information relevant to 2001, including photographs of laboratories, research vehicles, simulated docking and lunar landing devices, and film depicting appearance of man walking on the moon (simulator device). Considerable time spent in space station laboratory, viewing models and reports of space stations, and receiving briefings on rationale of space station technology.

Lear Siegler, Inc.
Grand Rapids, Michigan
Design concepts of advanced space vehicle instrumentation and display devices,

Food Technology Research Center, Libby, McNeil and Libby
Chicago, Illinois
Food selection and menus for long space voyages; basis of menu selection for the centrifuge.

Lick Observatory
Mt. Hamilton, California
Photography of the moon.

Ling-Temco-Vought, Inc.
Dallas, Texas
Reports on means and methods of displaying flight and other information to a crew undertaking an interplanetary space mission.

Lowell Observatory
Flagstaff, Arizona
Photography of the moon and planets.

Lunar and Planetary Laboratory, University of Arizona
Tucson, Arizona
Photography and charts of the moon.

Manned Spacecraft Center, National Aeronautics and Space Administration
Houston, Texas
Detailed photographic survey of the center; reports and miscellaneous technical documentation on many aspects of manned space flight, with particular emphasis on Apollo lunar spaceship and space station technology. Very valuable cooperation

in securing dozens of color photographs of the Earth taken from Mercury and Gemini spacecraft. Computer design and functioning; instrumentation; training techniques, astronaut routines, and conference room design and rationale utilized on lunar base sequence. MSC supplied six reels of Gemini tape in which mission control and pilot cross-talk was recorded. Maintenance and repair of space vehicles; Apollo mission rationale, time sequential analysis of crew activities and probable conversation with mission control, and advanced post-Apollo spacesuit design.

George C. Marshall Space Flight Center
National Aeronautics and Space Administration
Huntsville, Alabama
Detailed photographic survey of the Marshall Center, including manufacturing and test areas; design and utilization of display and recording instrumentations; design of advanced space vehicles; dozens of technical documents and photographs required during the film preparation.

Martin Co.
Baltimore, Maryland
Technical instrumentation.

Minnesota Mining & Manufacturing Co.
St. Paul, Minnesota
A broad program of cooperation was outlined at original meetings in St. Paul.

Mt. Wilson & Palomar Observatories
California Institute of Technology
Pasadena, California
Photography of the moon.

National Aeronautics and Space Administration Headquarters
Washington, D. C.
Space station philosophy, effects of rotation on man; speed of rotation. Photography made by Ranger lunar probes; photography of space vehicles and NASA facilities; photography of planet Mars, general and overall support from NASA; capabilities of man as scientific observers during deep space voyage; continuing documentation of myriad subjects throughout progress of film.

National Aeronautics and Space Council
Washington, D. C.
Feasibility of scene wherein a non-helmeted astronaut is very briefly exposed to space conditions.

National Institute of Medical Research
London, England
Hibernational techniques and instrumentation.

U. S. Naval Observatory
Flagstaff, Arizona

Elliott Automation, Ltd.
Borham Wood, Hertfordshire, England
Close support in supplying information on computer functions, readout materials, computer module design, computer terminology, and component miniaturization.

Individual (Don Flickinger, M.D., Gen. USAF, ret.)
Washington, D. C.
Appearance of the Earth from extreme altitudes.

Institute for Advanced Study, School of Mathematics
Princeton, New Jersey
Nuclear propulsion for Discovery.

Flight Research Center, National Aeronautics and Space Administration
Edwards, California
Lunar landing research vehicle design and operation. Design and utilization of Gemini spacesuits.

General Atomic-Division General Dynamics Corp.
San Diego, California
Propulsion system concepts for Discovery and capabilities of interplanetary spaceship.

General Dynamics-Convair
San Diego, California
Films on Mars manned exploration missions; trajectory studies on manned interplanetary missions; mission mode concepts; advanced spacesuit design.

General Electric Co., Missile and Space Division
Philadelphia, Pennsylvania
Design, instrumentation and rationale applicable to Space Station V lunar roving vehicles, lunar bus design, instrumentation applicable to lunar base design, rationale, console instrumentation and operation of Discovery's propulsion; this is the system actually used. Detailed description of system and instrumentation.

Goddard Space Flight Center
Greenbelt, Maryland
General support (1) surveying Goddard facility by photography; (2) photo and information files on spacecraft, tracking systems, computers, instrumentation consoles.

Grumman Aircraft Engineering Corp.
Bethpage, New York
Apollo LEM mockup, detailed guided review, including instrumentation panels. Apollo mission planning; flight profile; activities of crew during entire mission; communications, etc., all applicable to Aries IB and Orion.

Harbor General Hospital (A. T. K. Crockett, M.D., Chief of Urology)

Torrance, California
Consultation in the hibernation sequences, monitoring devices. Note: Crockett is co-author of the paper "Total Body Hypothermia for Prolonged Space Travel." Ideas incorporated to extend, as modified by Ormand Mitchell.

Hawker Siddeley Dynamics, Ltd.
Stevenage, Hertfordshire, England
Hawker Siddeley provided us the basic design of the interior of the space pods, including details of all the panels. They sent several experts to us on three or four occasions and a number of meetings were held at Stevenage with Clarke, Ordway, and Lange. They also aided us in antenna design and console instrumentation for antenna operation.

Honeywell, Inc.
Minneapolis, Minnesota
Assistance in instrumentation ranging from panels in Discovery and Pod Bay to the monitoring devices on the moon and the cockpit of Orion. Ideas were generated for the various docking sequences, leak detection aboard the Discovery, extravehicular activities, etc., etc. Honeywell prepared for us a special report entitled "A Prospectus for 2001 Interplanetary Flight." As for hardware, Honeywell provided us with many buttons and switches.

Illinois Institute of Technology, Research Institute
Chicago, Illinois

International Business Machines
Armonk, New York
S.K. received very broad and valuable support from IBM through the making of the film, ranging from the design and construction by IBM subcontractors of computer panels and consoles to the establishment of futuristic computer jargon and astronaut-computer interface. Also supplied valuable information on how computer-generated information would be displayed in future. Hardware contributions: panels for the Aries IB and the Orion cockpits plus buttons for many other sets, including Discovery's Command Module and centrifuge. IBM assigned Eliot Noyes & Associates, industrial designers (q.v.), as their consultants to work with us. Their personnel made several visits to the M-G-M studios in London during the course of making the film.

International Business Machines, Ltd.
London, England
IBM U.K. Ltd. provided the direct technical input to the IBM-built panels; see IBM entry and that of Eliot Noyes & Associates. IBM U.K. personnel visited the studios on a number of occasions, and many meetings were held in their offices.

Photography of the asteroids.

Office of Naval Research, Brand Office, Embassy of U. S. A.
London, England
Obtention of U.S. Navy full-pressure flight suit, including pressurization attachments, shoes, helmet; plus, technical documentation – all used in developing our own suits.

N. Y. U. College of Medicine
New York City
Development of techniques of placing man into hibernation and monitoring him when he is in the state. Very complete discussion of displays needed, design of the hibernaculums, a term devised by Dr. Ormand G. Mitchell, Assistant Professor of Anatomy, from whose many sketches were derived our final designs.

North American Aviation, Inc., Space and Information Systems Division
Downey, California
Photographs and documentation of the Apollo lunar spaceship. Simulated lunar base experimentations; nature of the lunar surface.

Eliot Noyes & Associates
New Canaan, Connecticut
Cooperation in design and rationale as appointed agents of IBM in all computer sequences for Aries IB and Orion, as well as spacesuit arm controls.

State of Oregon, Department of Geology & Mineral Information
Portland, Oregon
Extraction of useful resources from lunar surface materials, utilizing SNAP nuclear reactors as heat sources.

Paris Match
Paris, France
Supplied special futuristic cover for the magazine featured in Space Station V

Philco Corp.
Philadelphia, Pennsylvania
NASA-Manned Spacecraft Center Mission Control Center documentation, photography, and description of use of computer complex.

Royal Greenwich Observatory
Herstmonceux, Surrey, England
Design and rationale of the astronomical observatory and console in the centrifuge.

Societé de Prospection Electrique Schlumberger
Paris, France
Geophysical instrumentation for the centrifuge. Cooperation included a meeting in Paris, two trips by Schlumberger personnel to London, submission of design concepts and rationale for use.

Smithsonian Astrophysical Observatory
Cambridge, Massachusetts
Micrometeoroid danger to space flight; means of detection; nature of space in terms of Discovery's flight through the asteroids.

Soviet Embassy
London, England
Films of Soviet space programs. Stills of Luna 9 lunar photography.

United Kingdom Atomic Energy Authority,
Dorchester, England
Instrumentation of nuclear reactor control consoles in the centrifuge and in the Command Module. Meetings at Dragon reactor site and in studios.

University of London
Mill Hill, Hertfordshire, England
Advice on models of lunar surface; visit to studios and tour of laboratories at Mill Hill, including inspection of simulated lunar surface materials.

University of Manchester, Department of Astronomy
Manchester, England
Photography of the moon from Pic de Midi sources; large scale photos of Tycho and Clavius craters; charts and maps of many areas of the moon; consultation on surface characteristics of moon, nature of soil materials. Consultation on nature of celestial sphere as viewed from the Moon, i.e., the appearance of the heavens. Two meetings held in Manchester and one at the studios with members of Professor Kopal's staff.

University of Minnesota, School of Physics
Minneapolis, Minnesota
Extreme altitude conditions, appearance of Earth from high altitude balloons.

Vickers, Ltd., Medical Division
London, England
Advice on hibernation and health-monitoring equipment and techniques for the centrifuge.

U. S. Weather Bureau
Washington, D. C.
Detailed photographic coverage of the center; selection of documentation and photographs of appearance of Earth from satellite altitudes.

Whirlpool Corp., Systems Division
St. Joseph, Michigan
Development of the Aries IB kitchen and planning of eating programs and routines.

Let's look at a couple at random. North American Aviation's Space and Information Division in Downey California gave Kubrick "photographs and documentation of the Apollo lunar spaceship. Simulated lunar base experimentations; nature of the lunar surface." As I contend later in the book, even the Soviets contributed with "films of Soviet space programs. Stills of Lunar 9 photography."

"Capricorn 1" which was based on the initial edition of this book revealed how the motion picture aspects of the hoax were handled.

8

How Data Was Transmitted Worldwide

Once the Saturn was out of sight and until the capsule "returned", all evidence of the "flight" was in the form of electromagnetic waves. These, of course, are simple to simulate and transmit. Any or all of the four systems described below could have been employed. Others may have been used but these appear to be the most logical.

LEASED PHONE CONNECTIONS

The basic system was provided by direct wire connections interspersed with microwave transmissions. All were basically Bell System communications on a CIA basis: no monitors, or total "hands off" by the lessors.

At the input were, of course, the synchronized tape decks that provided the complete moon landing simulation. It should be noted that these included the response and "recommendations" of Mission Control at Houston. In other words, these tapes were not just transmissions from the moon —they included all audio and the simulated video from the moon set. Thus, Mission Control at Houston and all other communicators were speaking into essentially dead mikes.

Data sent into oscilloscopes, graphic recorders and TV screens showing data displays, computor recording banks, were all from this one master tape. Again, there could be no error since all events had been meticulously recorded even to the "boo-boos", jokes and seeming improvisations of the astronauts and their counterparts on earth. Experience for this masterful presentation was derived from the decades of sound track effort for both motion pictures and TV presentations of science fiction adventures.

LOW FREQUENCY TRANSMITTERS

Unknown to most Americans is the existence of an ultra-low frequency transmission station in a northwestern state. This facility is used to broadcast messages to submerged nuclear submarines. The radio waves sent by this station are so long they are lethal to humans if the latter are adjacent to the transmitter. This permits automatic security.

Also, the receivers are of special design and few amateurs would even dream of receiving this type of broadcast. Therefore, ULF was used as a backup to the other methods of transmitting Apollo simulation data of all types.

SATELLITE

The most sophisticated method was microwave satellite to microwave. As a backup, a special satellite contained a tape unit that could be triggered by the ASP control station at Mercury. Thus, there was redundance to the redundancy.

9

Murder By Negligence On Pad 34

"The fire hazard always existed and NASA, North American Aviation and everyone else connected with the Apollo program should have known it. Inside the command module were all three factors that could start a fire: frayed wiring, combustibles and, worst of all, pure oxygen that made the capsule an oxygen bomb."

—"Mission To The Moon"

Most historians of the Apollo era agree that the fire in the command capsule which killed Gus Grissom, Ed White and Roger Chaffee was a culmination of mis-management and negligence on the part of NASA. Although more than 20,000 instances of failure had been logged prior to this untimely disaster, it was this incident, the flaming death of three men, that finally focused worldwide attention on the shortcomings, errors and outright criminal behavior of NASA management.

It is obvious that NASA had a better public relations department than it did a safety division. The public had never been adequately warned of the impending disaster although there were many ominous mentions in the trade press. Aviation Week, Aerospace Technology and other magazines which the general public never reads, reported all events, good and bad. There were a few mentions in obscure journals such as this from the Columbia Journalism Review by J.A. Skardon: "Through 1966 and up to the time of the Apollo fire, there was a series of accidents which, if viewed as a pattern, could have alerted the press (and public) to a need for a thorough re-examination of the Apollo program."

And from the Journal of Spacecraft and Rockets, by F.J. Hendel of North American Aviation in mid-1964: "Oxygen is more important to the survival of man than food or water. On the other hand, it presents a fire hazard which is especially great on the launching pad when the cabin is pressurized with pure oxygen at more than atmospheric pressure. No fire-fighting methods have been developed that can cope with a fire in pure oxygen."

As "Mission To The Moon" cites: Neither NASA or NAA were prepared for a fire on the ground. Clearly the largest and most complex research and development program ever undertaken was far less than a perfect prototype for large-scale technological projects. Its decay had been spread ing like a slow systemic cancer for many years."

Our contention: if any agency of the government could not handle a relatively simple problem on the ground, how could it expect to handle a complex problem or problems in space?

Perhaps you'll wonder too after you read the actual word-for-word testimony that Baron gave to the Pad 34 fire investigating committee. These pages are reprinted from the actual government report. As you read, try to visualize the struggle of one solitary man against the tremendous power of the corporate-government hierarchy.

INVESTIGATION INTO APOLLO 204 ACCIDENT

STATEMENT OF THOMAS RONALD BARON

MR. TEAGUE. Will you give your full name and your address?

MR. BARON. Thomas Ronald Baron, 2856 Folsom Road, Mims, Fla.

MR. TEAGUE. Take just a few minutes and tell us something about your background.

MR. BARON. As far as my background goes, I have been in research and development for approximately the last 12 years. Four years of it in the Air Research Proving Ground in

Eglin Field, Fla., mostly in the research and development of subsystems of all the aircraft that we had up there which I think was mostly the U.S. Air Force inventory.

I have been in private business for some time in the past years in different trades, locksmithing work, approximately 3 years out of the last 10. I have been in high altitude research probes for Device Development Corp. out of Massachusetts for approximately 4 months in 1963. This took place also in Eglin Field.

I have been in the manufacturing of environmental test chambers primarily for use by NASA and the U.S. Navy and a little over 2 years on the North American Hound Dog program at Eglin Field as a calibration technician, console operator, and with the Apollo program since September 1965.

MR. TEAGUE. What is your educational background?

MR. BARON. Only high school.

MR. TEAGUE. Would you tell us where you were in the North American organization; just where did you fit, for example, with the safety plan for North American?

MR. BARON. I don't follow you, Mr. Chairman.

MR. TEAGUE. Just what was your job with North American?

MR. BARON. My task called out that I was a missile preflight inspector. My own particular tasks were quite varied, like many of the other inspectors. We were used quite often in other areas that we weren't familiar with because there was nobody else there to do the job and we were shifted around. I worked on the manned module, on the service module, on the water-glycol system for ground support.

I have worked in component testing of the environmental control system in the life support building. I have been over at the receiving section, warehouse section, inspecting parts coming in from vendors and going out to spacecraft and working sites.

I have worked in all the areas on the pads, pad 16, pad 34 —quite a roundabout area.

MR. TEAGUE. Mr. Baron, I have read your first report. I believe it was the 5-odd page report. I have listened to about 2½ hours of taped interviews of yours.

One of the statements you made was that noncertified items were placed in the spacecraft. The Review Board found that noncertified equipment items were installed in the command module at the time of test. It was testified in Washington that a number of these items were identified and known and were to be taken out before flight.

Of the items that you spoke of, do you know whether these were the same items that would have been taken out before flight?

MR. BARON. No, sir. I don't see how they could be actually taken out. Some of them were in the epoxy category and paint category and tape category. Possibly the tape could be removed. We use some tape for identification purposes in the Command Module which could be removed during flight.

MR. TEAGUE. Do you think the items you are speaking of are items which would have stayed in during flight if the capsule had flown?

MR. BARON. Yes.

MR. TEAGUE. You stated that North American had not lived up to their contractual obligations to the Government. Is that correct?

MR. BARON. I don't feel that they did; no, sir.

MR. TEAGUE. Mr. Baron, did you ever see their contract?

MR. BARON. No, sir; I have never seen it.

MR. TEAGUE. Will you tell us what you meant by that, what you had in mind?

MR. BARON. Well, there are certain things that a contractor has to comply with in my past experience, especially working with the Allentown Scientific Associates in Allentown, Pa. I was very familiar with the Government contracts, the basis of a lot of Government contracts as far as safety is concerned for personnel and working conditions and things of this nature.

This is primarily what I was talking about.

MR. TEAGUE. You were talking about safety and things that you have in your report?

MR. BARON. Yes. I believe most of the Government contracts read out as to safety pretty much the same.

MR. TEAGUE. Mr. Baron, either in your tape or in your

report, I don't remember which, you said you met a man in a grocery store who worked on the pad and who knew exactly what caused the fire, and he said others did.

MR. BARON. This is what he stated to me; yes, indeed.

MR. TEAGUE. Who was that man?

MR. BARON. Are you going to press me for that name?

MR. TEAGUE. Yes. We want to ask him about it.

MR. BARON. Very good. His name is Al Holmburg.

MR. TEAGUE. Who is he, do you know?

MR. BARON. Yes. sir. He is a spacecraft electronics technician.

MR. TEAGUE. That is a rather serious statement. We would like to ask him that question.

MR. BARON. Yes, sir, I realize it is a very serious statement.

MR. TEAGUE. Do you have any questions?

MR. GURNEY. Did you find out who the man worked for? Who did you say he was?

MR. BARON. Who his boss is, Mr. Gurney, I don't know. He is a spacecraft electronics technician.

MR. GURNEY. Does he work here?

MR. BARON. Yes, on this particular command module.

MR. GURNEY. Does he work for the Government or a contractor?

MR. BARON. North American Aviation.

MR. FULTON. When and where did he make the statement?

MR. BARON. He made the statement to me February 2 at a drugstore actually, in Titusville, Fla.

MR. FULTON. Do you know the name of the drugstore?

MR. BARON. Yes, sir. Cutler's Drugstore.

MR. FULTON. Who was there?

MR. BARON. No one was there—well, there were other customers in the area, but no one that we knew.

MR. FULTON. Was this a casual meeting?

MR. BARON. Yes.

MR. FULTON. You had known him before?

MR. BARON. Yes, sir.

MR. FULTON. Were you there for the purpose of talking this over?

MR. BARON. No, sir. It was an unintentional meeting.

MR. TEAGUE. He didn't tell you what he had in mind?

MR. BARON. No, sir.

MR. HECHLER. Is this the same man who told you that the astronauts tried for 5 minutes to get out of the capsule?

MR. BARON. Yes, sir, he did.

MR. HECHLER. Thank you.

MR. WYDLER. I know what you are doing is a very difficult thing and to try to put it in the best perspective we have, as Members of Congress, could you give us what you consider the most serious of your charges and summarize those for us?

I realize that this may not be possible. If so, explain and I will understand. I know you have made many specific points and so forth. I wonder if you could tell us from your own point of view what you think the most serious charges are and why. I would appreciate that if you could.

MR. BARON. Are you asking me what the actual source of all our trouble is?

MR. WYDLER. Well, if you want to express that, yes.

MR. BARON. I don't know if that is exactly what you are asking.

MR. WYDLER. I am really giving you a chance to tell us what you think. This is what I am offering to you. You can take the question the way you want. I am not trying to limit you in any particular way.

MR. BARON. Very well. It is quite varied as to what our problems are. As most people have said and realized, it is so extensive and covers so many areas it is difficult to believe that some of them even existed. I would say basically that we have had problems, extensive problems in safety, in cleaning materials, in items getting in the spacecraft that weren't supposed to be there, the morale of the people, the pressures put on the people by management are the things that really indicate that we don't have the proper management that we should have in this program.

MR. WYDLER. That is all well and good and those are a

conclusion. I am sure you realize people disagree about things of that nature, and you can make an argument for and against it.

MR. BARON. Yes.

MR. WYDLER. And I am sure you realize how people can go back and forth on that.

MR. BARON. Sure.

MR. WYDLER. Tell me what you consider to be the most serious deficiencies you can point to as a matter of fact and tell me what they are from your point of view.

MR. BARON. This would be going into detail on some points?

MR. WYDLER. Pick out what you would consider to be the most significant of those points.

MR. BARON. I would have to go back and read my manuscript again, it is quite long.

I would say probably that the—I don't know if I am answering your question again, I don't even entirely understand it. Probably the lack of communication between almost everyone concerned with this project and the sectionalism that exists in this particular project is probably our main problem.

By this I mean if I were to write a letter about a particular instance or a fire or something like this or something we have had and try to get it up through channels, it would be stopped along the way.

This has occurred not only to me, it has occurred to other individuals in quality control, also. The communication going up is very, very poor and the communication coming down is very, very poor.

MR. WYDLER. Do you have some specific illustrations of that fact which you consider the most significant illustrations of that?

MR. BARON. I don't believe that there is any most significant illustration of it, because there are too many of them and you couldn't possibly pick one out of the others. If you want to pick out an instance on a particular problem that I have written about or covered, then I could possibly do that.

MR. WYDLER. I am asking you to pick one out.

MR. BARON. Okay, I am going to give one instance which goes into the communications problem literally during the escape operation, this is the self-contained apparatus that we have for working with the toxic fuels, the nitrogen tetroxide and nitrogen hydrazenes during the filling of our tanks, this is not in relation to spacecraft 012; it is spacecraft 9. It was a general problem at that time.

We did not have a good communication link with the people that were actually in control of us and our air pax during the entire operation. We had too many communications breaks, we couldn't talk to them in case somebody got hurt. If a man got out of air we had to get him down ourselves and in most cases, we would be walking back to the escape trailer which is operated by another contractor, Bendix, before the truck would even get out to assist us in any way.

This is primarily because we didn't have any good headest communication between them or they were not on the net and talking to somebody else.

MR. WYDLER. Thank you, Mr. Chairman.

MR. TEAGUE. Mr. Fulton.

MR. FULTON. Of course when you are testifying, you are giving your word. Naturally, the inquiry then results as to corroboration of your word, so my first question is after the meeting with this Al Holmburg, has he contacted you or have you contacted him since, and if so, how, when, and where?

MR. BARON. Yes; I have contacted him several times, on several occasions since this accident.

MR. FULTON. In connection with this accident?

MR. BARON. Yes.

MR. FULTON. Did he, on his own motion, try to contact you after you made these statements either confirming or denying what you had said he had stated?

MR. BARON. No, sir; he made no direct attempt ever to contact me.

MR. FULTON. This committee, of course, wants a clear and fair examination of the facts. You have cited certain events that have occurred with other people involved.

Do you have recommendations to this committee of a person or persons or a company or a supplier or a systems engineer that we should contact to corroborate what you say? What corroboration can you give us that what you say is true? How shall we do that?

MR. BARON. You mean aside from Mr. Holmburg?

MR. FULTON. Yes.

MR. BARON. Well—

MR. FULTON. You have given other instances. We are listening to your words. The question is whether the committee should take them on their face value. We need to know who you recommend to us to corroborate what you say? Is it a company? individuals? engineers? systems engineers? Who is it? Pad operations people?

MR. BARON. Well, in reference to Mr. Holmburg's statement to me, I would suggest that you talk to Mr. Holmburg.

Mr. FULTON. Oh, we clearly will do that. But you have clearly given many other instances. The question is, How do we corroborate these other instances on what you say? Who shall we get in touch with and put our investigators to check so that it corroborates your statements?

MR. BARON. Yes, sir; if you will give me the instances you have in mind, I will be more than happy to.

MR. FULTON. All or any of them. Do you know of anybody that this committe has not called as a witness whom you could recommend we call to corroborate what you say?

MR. WYDLER. Would the gentlemen yield to me?

MR. FULTON. I couldn't on that. I would rather have him answer that.

Mr. BARON. Yes, sir. I can give you a list of their names if I have a list of the North American personnel because of the names I don't recall.

MR. TEAGUE. There are a number of names in your report.

MR. BARON. May I pull my report out? I will be glad to read them.

MR. FULTON. Is Robert Lucas one?

MR. BARON. Yes.

MR. FULTON. Would you suggest we call him?

MR. BARRON. He would certainly have to corroborate what I said in relation to him.

MR. FULTON. Who else?

MR. BARON. A mechanic by the name of Donald Butcher could verify that particular item I am discussing here.

MR. FULTON. Who else?

MR. BARON. William Aimerson.

MR. FULTON. You have a list here on the water-glycol operations and you have given us the names of ground support people, Mel Gill, Bill Aimerson, Chuck Levitt, Dennis Jolly, Bill de Jurnat, Sam Moody, Ed Wright of NASA, and Jerry Dahl of Air Research. What do you say about those people?

MR. BARON. If you talk to either one, they will have to corroborate what I have said, because what I have said in the report is certainly true. They were there in most instances in all those cases, that I have written about.

MR. FULTON. To whom did you report the statement by Mr. Holmburg? That was a serious statement, as you realized, regarding the cause of this accident. To whom did you make such a report and when did you do it?

MR. BARON. I discussed it with a newspaperman, this particular report.

MR. FULTON. Who was it?

MR. BARON. Sanders Lamont, of Today newspaper, or possibly Dick Younger, of Orlando Sentinel.

MR. FULTON. You didn't go to NASA and you didn't come to Congress or the Review Board which had been appointed to investigate the accident directly?

MR. BARON. I am trying to recall whether or not I discussed this with John Brooks, of NASA. In fact, I may have on one occasion, because I did discuss with him what Mr. Holmburg was discussing with me.

MR. FULTON. What is his title?

MR. BARON. He is a quality control regional investigator.

MR. WYDLER. Would the gentlemen yield to me for just an instant?

MR. FULTON. I will be glad to.

MR. WYDLER. As I understand the testimony that the committee received in Washington, the North American Aviation Co., which has reviewed your specific charges in great detail obviously, testified that you are about half right. That was their testimony, so we can assume from that you are probably at least half right. There is some basis, obviously, for the things you have said and charged. I think that is part of our record in Washington.

MR. FULTON. May I comment on that? I make no assumptions as to whether he is right or wrong. I want the corroboration and the people who will support his testimony as well as the physical facts that I think we should go into. That is what I was calling to the witness's attention, what must this committee do to corroborate what he said.

I make no assumption to whether or not he is right or wrong in whole or in part.

MR. TEAGUE. Mr. Gurney.

MR. GURNEY. Mr. Baron, you mentioned something about the morale factor in connection with the people who are working on the Apollo program or here in the spaceport in general.

Let us amplify that a bit. How would you describe this morale?

MR. BARON. The morale as of less than 3 weeks ago was very, very poor and I have never seen the morale since the time I have been with the company at what anyone would call a normal high point at all.

In other words, you could possibly say it was a "blah" feeling among the people as far as the morale is concerned.

MR. GURNEY. This is a serious matter. The morale of people working, whether it is good or bad, certainly reflects in the quality of their work. Be more specific. What do you mean by poor? In what way?

MR. BARON. In two cases in regard to morale on space-craft 9 and spacecraft 11, there has been or there were cases of people who were shifted to different shifts prior to the launch of these two separate vehicles. In the case of space-craft 9, the people did not get the pay benefits which would normally happen if they were transferred to another shift.

In the case of spacecraft 11, some of the people got these benefits and some of the people did not.

MR. GURNEY. But, again, going back to a morale question, it is a difficult thing to assess. You know, in the Army, and most of us here spent some time in the service one way or another, we often said that if a soldier wasn't "bitching real loud" as we put it, there was something the matter with him. Actually this sort of thing goes on a good deal. There is morale, and morale. People do get upset and they complain.

But I am saying, do you think that there was a really serious morale factor with people generally dissatisfied all over the place with their jobs and what they are doing?

MR. BARON. I would say for the most part yes, and I would be more than happy to give you other names of people that you can talk to.

MR. GURNEY. Who would they be?

MR. BARON. Mr. Wade McCrary, who is no longer with us—these are North American people who have left us—Mr. Myron Cross, Mr. Al Miller, Mr. Jack Berger—I think Mr. Berger is still with us, I don't know for sure. Mr. Dick Menthorn—if I had a list in front of me, I could really reel them all off to you, but this is what I have on the top of my head right now.

MR. GURNEY. Of those who have left, do you know where they have gone?

MR. BARON. Yes, sir.

MR. GURNEY. Where?

MR. BARON. Mr. Cross is working for Grumman. Mr. McCrary and Miller are working for Lockheed.

MR. GURNEY. That is here?

MR. BARON. Yes, sir. In this area.

MR. GURNEY. What would you say was the chief reason for this lack of morale, as you put it?

MR. BARON. Well, I think basically personnel treatment and how some of them were treated and just in general as far as overtime was concerned; a case in point is two particular instances when I called in because I was not feeling well and actually not up to par for working, I called in two particular afternoons that I was going to stay home that particular day, because I wasn't feeling well, and I almost was demended to go to work, and that I would work—especially since I was the only one in that particular area that was working; this was in the receiving and inspection area.

MR. GURNEY. The morale factor is connected only with the North American Corp. Are there others involved?

MR. BARON. Not that I know of. It is primarily North American.

MR. TEAGUE. Mr. Gurney.

MR. GURNEY. What about NASA people? Are they involved?

MR. BARON. I have never really seen them in too bad of a morale picture at all. They are not contractor workers, they are Government workers. [Laughter.]

MR. GURNEY. Why do you make this distinction? [Laughter.]

MR. BARON. Well, for the most part, naturally NASA is supposed to be the controlling outfit in this organization and usually if a quality control inspector—well, normally he is put on the spot in many cases as to whether he is going to buy something or what, and then NASA—the NASA man will turn around and argue the point and either go or not go with him. I would consider they are one notch higher mostly, and they don't concern our morale problem.

MR. GURNEY. With respect again to the morale, you identified the poor quality of the morale, as you put it, due to shifts in jobs and uncertainty in jobs. Is that the sort of thing you are talking about?

MR. BARON. Yes; actually it is. One case in point again after Spacecraft 9 was launched, we were supposed to have a shift rotation on a man-for-man basis and for the most part this did not come about, and it was difficult to get transferred to another shift. I myself was on a second shift for well over a year. There were many reasons why I wasn't put on the first shift, because somebody else was going to school, or some such reason as that. We were limited as to our amount of people.

The person was left in the area in that particular spot and he just stayed there.

Some of these shift changes were actually put in the desk drawer and forgotten about.

MR. GURNEY. You mean a request for a shift change?

MR. BARON. No; the manager supervision, one supervisor made an attempt to get people's names and what shifts they wanted to go to, but that was usually as far as it ever went.

MR. GURNEY. Are you saying that it didn't reach the top, is that the idea?

MR. BARON. I couldn't know right now whether it reached the top or it reached the top and it was just shut off or whatever. This problem is supposed to be still in existence now.

MR. GURNEY. Are there any particular groups of workers that you would say were particularly affected by poor morale as you call it?

MR. BARON. Well, in relation to the receiving and inspection area at North American, we had several people in there, in fact all the people in there, that were working there in August and September and October this last year, I don't know any of them that wanted to stay in. They were all trying to get out but I guess they were corralled in that particular area and that is where they stayed. They were not actually receiving inspectors.

MR. GURNEY. Was this because they didn't like that particular kind of a job?

MR. BARON. Well the receiving inspector job is a labor grade 6 or 8 or possibly 10 and many of us were top 12 in a particular area and just didn't have any business being there really, where our job codes called for other jobs, although this is a vital area.

MR. GURNEY. But nothing wrong with the treatment of the people who are doing this kind of job?

MR. BARON. Well, I think if you had an interview with Mr. Wade McCrary about treatment of people, I believe he will give you a better answer on the subject. He was supposedly acting leadman for quite some time and had the responsibility of acting leadman and when he finally challenged the management for his job for leaderman, he was not made leadman, so he left the company.

MR. GURNEY. One final question; assuming what you say about morale is true, do you think this affected the work on the job?

MR. BARON. Yes, sir; I do.

MR. GURNEY. In what way?

MR. BARON. Well, especially in reference to safety, lackadaisical in some job operations, sleeping on the job, people just—a lot of them just didn't care one way or the other and I am not talking about isolated instances, many times of bookreading and sleeping and things of this nature.

MR. GURNEY. That is all.

MR. TEAGUE. Mr. Daddario?

MR. DADDARIO. Mr. Baron, as I take it from the response to Mr. Gurney's question, you certainly were personally unhappy with the situation.

MR. BARON. Well, I don't know what you mean by personally unhappy.

MR. DADDARIO. You were testifying as to the morale of others. How did this affect you, individually?

MR. BARON. Well, I didn't feel too well about the other people being treated and myself being treated as we were being treated. I have had a health problem for some time on this particular contract as a diabetic and it was supposedly difficult for me to work many of the long hours that I did have to work.

MR. DADDARIO. This same characteristic that you apply to others, you agree to, and that there was a bad general overall condition amongst the North American employees?

MR. BARON. Yes, sir.

MR. DADDARIO. Yet, in your report which I have before me, when your work was terminated with North American you said, "I was terminated at 4 o'clock that evening. It was a very sorrowful event for me. There was nothing more that I wanted than to be associated with the space program."

MR. BARON. That is correct.

MR. DADDARIO. How do you tie that in with your previous statements?

MR. BARON. Which previous statements?

MR. DADDARIO. Why would it have been a sorrowful event to leave a program that you wanted to be associated with if, in fact, the conditions under which you were working were so terrible as you indicated them to be in answer to Mr. Gurney's question?

MR. BARON. Regardless of whether or not North American Aviation treated its people properly, you would still have a job to do and the bird is up there, and the people are up there, and you have a task to perform.

MR. DADDARIO. What was your job?

MR. BARON. I was a quality control inspector.

MR. DADDARIO. What did that include and involve?

MR. BARON. An extensive amount of responsibilities.

MR. DADDARIO. Well, "extensive," sir, is something that is hard for me to comprehend under these circumstances.

MR. BARON. Yes, sir.

MR. DADDARIO. You had a job as a missile preflight inspector.

MR. BARON. That is what is on my particular record.

MR. DADDARIO. What were your hours of employment and what were you supposed to be doing during those hours?

MR. BARON. When I was a foreman my hours of employment varied tremendously. They normally were 3:30 in the afternoon until midnight. I usually reported to work approximately 1 hour early and in some cases—well, in many cases in the past year or so we have worked 55 and 60-hour weeks. My job included verifying proper installation of components, verifying that tests were being run per procedure or documented changes, verifying the proper identification and damage of materials going into the spacecraft and out to the sites to be used in the ground support work.

MR. DADDARIO. Where did you do that?

MR. BARON. What?

MR. DADDARIO. Where did you work?

MR. BARON. Locationwise, I worked at pad 34 on the

complex and on the gantry. I have worked at pad 16, which is prepressure test facility, propulsion test facility. I have worked in the life support area, I have worked in receiving inspection, I have worked in the site lab or computer room, as we call it. It is a test troubleshooting area, and I have worked at the MSOB right here at the high bay area on the floor.

MR. DADDARIO. You didn't feel that was a proper designation for the work that you were doing? You should have had another designation?

MR. BARON. It all depends on what outline the personnel will give you for labor grade 12.

MR. DADDARIO. You said you were an LG-12, but that you shouldn't have been there. Even though you were designated as that, you should have been something else. I wonder what idea you had in mind with reference to your classification?

MR. BARON. I think in reference to that it was when I was describing my work at launch complex 34. At that time I was not a top labor grade 12. It was just several months or a couple months after I was hired by the company and in some cases the water glycol engineer would leave the net, then I would be the only one on the net as far as the blockhouse participant was concerned.

MR. DADDARIO. You felt that you should have had a higher classification and greater responsibility?

MR. BARON. No, sir. I felt someone else should be there with more authority. A labor grade 12 is at the bottom and doesn't have hardly any authority, and to be left in his hands shouldn't occur.

MR. DADDARIO. Was it a matter of authority or competency and experience? Did you feel you had experience to do the job?

MR. BARON. Yes, sir; I did.

MR. DADDARIO. You were dissatisfied, not with the job being properly done on that occasion, because you felt that you personally had the competence. But you did not have the job classification and authority to go along with it?

MR. BARON. No. That is negative. I felt that the

engineer who was in charge of the test should have stayed on the test, either he or his NASA counterpart, of which there was no one.

MR. DADDARIO. You worked at North American for how long?

MR. BARON. On the Apollo program since September 20, 1965.

MR. DADDARIO. You started out in what capacity?

MR. BARON. At the bottom of labor grade 12.

MR. DADDARIO. You continued in that capacity during the course of your employment with them, until terminated?

MR. BARON. No, sir. I was promoted until I got to the top of labor grade 12.

MR. DADDARIO. During the course of your employment with North American you proceeded from a low level 12 to the top level 12. Were you properly promoted within that period of time?

MR. BARON. Yes, sir.

MR. HECHLER. Mr. Chairman.

MR. TEAGUE. Mr. Hechler.

MR. HECHLER. Mr. Baron, the Board of Review very meticulously examined the events leading up to the fire and the Board conclusively repudiates the allegation that you have carried to this committee that the astronauts tried for five minutes to get out of the spacecraft, and this committee heard the last 6 minutes of tape which, in itself, repudiates this allegation, and I think it is utterly irresponsible for you to come before this committee and attempt to dignify a conversation that you had in a drugstore in an effort to set forth conclusions which have been repudiated by a very thorough examination of a Board review. I feel it is unfortunate that this has been brought before the committee.

I think this report of the Review Board speaks for itself. I would just like to ask one or two very brief questions.

Do you know who Mr. Slayton is, Mr. Baron?

MR. BARON. Yes, sir; I know who he is.

MR. HECHLER. Do you know what position he holds in the space program?

MR. BARON. Well, not exactly.

MR. HECHLER. You don't know what position he holds in the space program?

MR. BARON. You mean direct connection with it?

MR. HECHLER. Yes.

MR. BARON. I think I know what he is; yes, sir. But I don't know his title.

MR. HECHLER. Do you know what his first name is?

MR. BARON. Yes, sir—well, no, sir; I only know and refer to him as "Deke."

MR. HECHLER. Do you know how he spells his last name?

MR. BARON. Yes.

MR. HECHLER. How does he spell his last name?

MR. BARON. S-l-a-y-t-o-n, I believe.

MR. HECHLER. Thank you.

I observed on three or four different occasions you spelled it a different way in the report, and I just felt that wasn't very good quality control at that point.

Thank you, Mr. Chairman.

MR. TEAGUE. Mr. Fulton.

MR. FULTON. The question arises on your opportunity to observe and your qualifications for observation. You were hired by North American as a labor grade 12, and stayed within that class all during your service since September 20, 1965, is that correct?

MR. FULTON. That is not in a professional nor engineering category, but a labor category; is it not?

MR. BARON. What do you classify as labor?

MR. FULTON. It is a nontechnical qualified engineering or nonprofessional position; is that not right?

MR. BARON. No, sir; I think it calls for technically qualified people, but not anyone with an engineering degree.

MR. FULTON. Therefore from your previous experience and education you are not qualified to give an expert opinion on engineering processes or systems. Is that correct?

MR. BARON. No, sir; that is not correct.

If I see a particular indication that is improper, whether or not an engineer agrees with it, it may be wrong. This has occurred on many occasions where engineering itself has argued the point. I have won many arguments on this point, and engineering has.

Testing out these vehicles and systems is no more complicated than running a field quality check on an old B-52 bomber. I was an airman second class, nontechnical, nonengineering type when I was doing that kind of work.

MR. FULTON. Is the basis of your criticism in the engineering procedures either —

MR. BARON. Would you repeat that question, please?

MR. FULTON. I will ask the reporter to read the question to you.

THE REPORTER. I didn't understand the question, either. Would you be good enough to repeat it? [Laughter.]

MR. FULTON. Is your criticism either of NASA or North American directed at engineering procedures or systems?

I don't believe it is, is it?

MR. BARON. In some cases it is, on the water glycol system.

MR. FULTON. Now, the other point that I would like to inquire into is your ability to observe or whether your observations might be colored by your own personal reasons or motives. You have spoken that you have physical difficulties. What were those physical difficulties during this time of employment?

MR. BARON. Mostly from overwork and not being able to go home.

MR. FULTON. Well, those are the reasons, but what were the difficulties?

MR. BARON. Well, exhaustion would be one of them, tiredness.

MR. FULTON. Were you under the care of a physician or physicians, a chiropractor or a psychiatrist at any time during this period?

MR. BARON. Which period, sir?

MR. FULTON. Of your employment since September 20, 1965, under North American.

MR. BARON. I have been under a doctor's care quite often.

MR. FULTON. Who were the doctors?

MR. BARON. Dr. Chastain of the Jess Parish Hospital, or the Titusville clinic, here.

MR. FULTON. For what did you see him?

MR. BARON. Nervous condition.

MR. FULTON. Is he a doctor or a psychiatrist?

MR. BARON. He is a doctor, a doctor of internal medicine, I believe.

MR. FULTON. How many times did you see him over this period for a nervous condition?

MR. BARON. I saw him on one day. He was an associate of Dr. Osmond who was treating me as a diabetic and an ulcer.

MR. FULTON. You have had an ulcer during this time?

MR. BARON. Yes, sir, I most certainly did.

MR. FULTON. Could your complaints have been caused by the condition of your ulcer acting on your own feelings?

MR. BARON. No, sir. I think Dr. Chastain could possibly verify that the only reason I got the nervous and ulcer condition was that I was concerned with spacecraft 12.

MR. FULTON. What other doctor had you seen and for what purpose?

MR. BARON. Prior to that time, Dr. Blackburn in the Melbourne General Hospital in Melbourne, Fla.

MR. FULTON. What for?

MR. BARON. Diabetes.

MR. FULTON. Who else did you see?

MR. BARON. A Dr. Killinger at the Holiday Hospital in Orlando during Christmas of last year when I was in the hospital.

MR. FULTON. Why did you see him?

MR. BARON. It was for a diabetes problem.

MR. FULTON. Was it anything to do with any problems that caused physical stress on you and your mind?

MR. BARON. Yes, sir. This is one of the reasons why my diabetes at this particular time was going off kilter, I guess you could say.

MR. FULTON. Who else did you see during this period?

MR. BARON. During my hospital stay, you mean, aside from doctor—

MR. FULTON. How long were you there? We are trying to get your medical history to see what power you had to observe.

MR. WYDLER. Would it be possible for Mr. Baron to submit it for the record? We don't want to listen to every doctor he has ever seen in his life.

MR. FULTON. I want to know if his observations were made from a capacity which is unbiased or uncolored by his physical condition. I think that information would contribute to the hearing. Would you quickly give me another one or two?

MR. BARON. That is all the doctors I had seen lately. I talked to Dr. Hare, the astronauts' doctor, I believe, or one of them on the staff.

MR. FULTON. Was that for a physical condition or a mental condition?

MR. BARON. I wouldn't know. It was after the inquiry board hearing. And I took it as a psychiatric examination.

MR. FULTON. Was there any report given on that?

MR. BARON. No, sir, not that I know of.

MR. FULTON. Was it an extensive examination?

MR. BARON. No, sir, it was a half-hour conversation with him about problems on the spacecraft, and I believe he went into some personal things also.

MR. FULTON. Your problems, too?

MR. BARON. That is correct.

MR. FULTON. So that both you and your mind and the spacecraft had problems, didn't you?

MR. BARON. I think we all have our own problems. [Laughter.]

The spacecraft definitely had its problems.

MR. FULTON. That is all.

MR. TEAGUE. Mr. Baron, if things were really as bad as you pictured them by the things that you have said to this committee in your report, do you believe we would ever have gotten a shot off to the moon? Do you think we ever would have had one successful shot?

MR. BARON. Certainly, sir.

MR. TEAGUE. With the conditions you pictured here, do you think we could be successful in any of our shots?

MR. BARON. No, sir; no, sir; I don't think so.

MR. TEAGUE. We have had a lot of successes?

MR. BARON. Yes, sir; you have. But not on the Apollo program.

MR. TEAGUE. Mr. Wydler.

MR. WYDLER. I just want to get very clear about that one doctor that you told us about. You say that a doctor from NASA talked to you about something or other. How did that come about? Did you ask to see them, or did he request you to talk to him, or what?

MR. BARON. Mr. Wydler, since I discussed this report with the first man I ever met in the hospital back in November, I had a NASA man in the hospital with me over here as a roommate for a 24-hour period. I had a NASA man in the Orlando hospital talk to me about the same problems I am discussing right now.

When I was transferred over there he showed up the next day and talked to me for 2 days. I also saw Mr. John Brooks over at the Orlando hospital. He was an investigator from Washington headquarters in NASA. He held an interview with me over there. When I got back home after the accident had occurred, I was called to meet with the inquiry board. I believe there was nine of them there, one of the subboards, and Dr. Hare was there also, and he wanted to have a half hour or so private session with me after the board left, which he did have, and he indicated to me certainly that he was delving into personal problems of my own, asking me about them—well, it was another case of a NASA man talking to me about the same problems.

MR. WYDLER. Did he say he was acting on anybody's behalf or on NASA's behalf, or on the review board's behalf?

MR. BARON. No, sir. Only one NASA man, Mr. Brooks, said this. No one said they were acting on behalf of any board.

MR. WYDLER. Let me understand this. Do all these matters of deficiencies, as you express them in this program, relate directly to matters of safety? I know in a broad sense they all relate to safety. But, if you can tell us, do any of them relate to matters of what we would call immediate safety to the crew of the spacecraft?

MR. BARON. No, sir.

MR. WYDLER. Let me ask you one final question: You know, exhibit A here is the picture I had asked some questions about to the witnesses from NASA and North American that were here just before you. Do you know anything about the wire which is theorized to be the wire that is guilty of causing this fire? Do you know anything regarding its installation, its inspection, or anything that might throw some light on this particular wire, the lithium door, or anything of that nature?

MR. BARON. Yes, sir, I do. But, here, again, it is something that has been referred to me by another individual, and if I do bring it up, I dislike being called irresponsible in making any of these comments to you. People have to understand, especially this committee, that these people could not say anything to anybody about this thing when it did occur. I happened to have been terminated the day I got back to work. I wasn't out for allowing these people here—I got a lot of anonymous calls from people about troubles on the spacecraft prior and immediately prior to the fire. These people that I discussed it with knew they were jeopardizing their jobs if they were caught talking to me or discussing something they got out of the news. This is how the company feels about it, naturally.

MR. WYDLER. You are saying you don't know anything about this personally, but you are indicating somebody might have said something to you about it; is that right?

MR. BARON. Definitely.

MR. WYDLER. You don't feel that you want to discuss that with the committee at this time?

MR. BARON. I would be more than happy to say it, if Mr. Hechler would take a more objective view of the statements.

MR. WYDLER. I can't answer for Mr. Hechler, but I would like to hear it.

MR. BARON. Yes, sir; I will be more than happy to.

MR. WYDLER. Please tell us.

MR. BARON. I discussed it with another individual at his home, and he witnessed one evening when he was working three technicians who were supposed to flush out, this is by purging the environmental control unit with an alcohol solution to apparently clean it and get it ready for proper use. He disclosed to me that a 55-gallon drum had been delivered to the site, I guess it was right here at MSOB. I don't know for sure. I guess it was—a 55-gallon drum of 190-proof alcohol that was delivered to them.

The three men who were assigned to flushing this unit out were—well, one of them took a 5-gallon jug of this stuff home and one other, or perhaps all three of them, I don't really recall right now, had mixed this stuff and cut it with water and were drinking it right here at the site, and they were carrying it around in plastic bags.

MR. WYDLER. Well, that doesn't have anything to do with this particular wire or this particular door.

MR. BARON. Possibly so, because they were working on that unit and the spacecraft, and this is the only link I would put between them, between what you have there and the drinking.

MR. FULTON. Would you yield?

I want to say who, when, and where?

MR. WYDLER. I just want to finish this up, if I could Mr. Baron, I notice one other thing under life support you pointed out in your report. It is our report of your report, on page 17. It does relate to spacecraft 12, and you were talking about the fuel tank being worked on without any paperwork and so forth. Would this have anything to do with the wire or lithium door that we are talking about here?

MR. BARON. No, sir.

MR. WYDLER. That is all.

MR. FULTON. When you are speaking about people, it naturally raises the question, who, when, and where. Who was there to observe with you?

MR. BARON. The same gentleman is Mr. Holmburg that disclosed that information to me. That is the only name I know. And I have related to Mr. Wydler exactly what he related to me.

MR. FULTON. This Mr. Holmburg was not involved in this situation, was he? He was simply the relay of hearsay of what went on, wasn't he?

MR. BARON. That is right, sir.

MR. FULTON. I would like to make clear that this committee has no official position with regard to you nor have I said anything favorably or unfavorably about your testimony. I certainly want to inquire and get corroboration so we can determine the correctness and the truth of your statements. If you will cooperate with this committee, and with the chairman's permission, put into the record any further suggestions of witnesses, times, or events we can look into, outside of the report, which we have all read, please let us hear.

MR. BARON. Which report was that, sir?

MR. FULTON. The original report.

MR. BARON. I have sent to the chairman of this committee a more thorough report which includes all the names.

MR. FULTON. I have all the names, but I read them and said to myself, who should we call?

MR. BARON. No, sir. You are talking about the 55-page report. I am talking about the 500-page report.

MR. TEAGUE. Your report went to the chairman of the full committee, not to me. He told me he received it.

MR. BARON. I have a 500-page report. I have an opening statement which I wanted to read, which described this 500-page report, and in this I think you can get all the possible names that there are, the times, the dates, the tests that were being run and the internal letters of the company, proper specifications, especially in regard to flammability of materials. All this is in this new report.

MR. FULTON. When did you start to take such a serious and active interest in what you felt was wrong and kept such detailed records? Why did you do it? Why didn't you refer it to someone else within your company who had responsibility to investigate?

MR. BARON. This was done. I started working for this company in September 1965. I started taking notes in November of 1965 when I was assigned to the pad 34 complex. All my daily notes and many, many more letters and reports I had made out were sent up through my headman and through assistant supervision. If they did not get through to the top, then I don't know what happened to the notes and letters. But they were sent up.

The information in either of my reports were given to North American on a time-to-time basis, on a daily basis, practically. I used to run my supervisor out of these forms because I had so many letters, because I used to write so many of these letters about discrepant actions.

MR. FULTON. Did other people who were working with you do this, too, or were you the only one?

MR. BARON. I don't believe anybody did it to the extent that I did it, sir.

MR. FULTON. That is all, sir.

MR. WYDLER. Could I suggest that if Mr. Baron has some concluding remarks, or if he would like to submit a statement for the record, that he may be afforded an opportunity? I see you have something before you, and perhaps you would like to put it in.

MR. BARON. I think I have covered most of it. I have the report that I would like to be submitted as a part of the record, the 500-page report.

MR. WYDLER. That means printing it. That is something we should leave to the committee, something of that length, whether we want to print it as part of the public documents. We can take it as an exhibit. Whether we will print it as part of the public record is something we should decide after we see it.

Is that all right with you?

MR. BARON. Yes.

MR. TEAGUE. I think we are through with you. The Board has found some of the things you have said to be true. What you have done has caused North American to search their procedures.

Thank you very much.

MR. BARON. Thank you.

MR. TEAGUE. Mr. Holmburg, are you in the room?

(Whereupon, Mervin Holmburg was called before the committee, and, being first duly sworn, was examined and replied as follows:)

MR. TEAGUE. Mr. Holmburg, did you come here of

your own free will?

MR. HOLMBURG. Yes, sir.

MR. TEAGUE. Would you give us your full name and address for the sake of the record?

MR. HOLMBURG. Mervin Holmburg, 3031 Pimbrook Road, Titusville, Fla.

MR. TEAGUE. Mr. Holmburg, Mr. Baron has testified, as I am sure you know, that you told him that you knew what caused the accident and all about it. Did you ever tell him anything of that nature?

MR. HOLMBURG. No, sir.

MR. FULTON. Will you put your hand down away from your mouth?

MR. TEAGUE. Did you ever discuss the cause of the accident in a drugstore with Mr. Baron?

MR. HOLMBURG. No. I talked to him many times in the drugstore, but that is about it.

MR. TEAGUE. But you did not say that you and other people know what caused the fire?

MR. HOLMBURG. No, sir.

MR. DADDARIO. What was the nature of your conversation with him on those occasions in the drugstore?

MR. HOLMBURG. Well, most of them was about his report, why he wrote it and when he wrote it and so forth. Whether he was making progress on it.

MR. DADDARIO. Did you in any instance while he was relating this to you agree with him as to the difficulties which the Apollo spacecraft had run into and the tragedy that had occurred which would give him any indication that you did have the answer to the problem which caused the fire?

MR. HOLMBURG. Never.

MR. DADDARIO. Can you say that with as clear a recollection as possible of the conversation you had with Mr. Baron?

MR. HOLMBURG. Yes, sir. I bumped into him accidentally almost every time I met him. I told him I shouldn't even be talking with him because of the report he is writing, and he is probably being watched. He gets all his information from anonymous phone calls, people calling him and people dropping him a word here and there. That is what he tells me.

MR. DADDARIO. What caused you to come here today? We had not scheduled you as a witness. I had no idea; in fact, I can't recall that I ever heard your name before today. What brought you here?

MR. HOLMBURG. Well, I work right outside the door here, and it is my time to come to work now.

MR. DADDARIO. Why would you have asked that you might be allowed to testify?

MR. HOLMBURG. Well, Mr. Baron had brought my name up a couple of times in here, and I thought I should come in here to defend it.

MR. DADDARIO. You come here for that purpose?

MR. HOLMBURG. Yes, sir.

MR. WYDLER. Who told you that?

MR. HOLMBURG. I can't recall who that was now.

MR. WYDLER. You mean you can't recall who told you that?

MR. HOLMBURG. There were several people right outside the door and I overheard it being mentioned.

MR. SMART. I am Mr. Robert Smart, Assistant to the President of North American Aviation.

When Mr. Holmburg's name was injected into this testimony in the manner in which all of you know, I did not feel that we could leave it unanswered at this time, if there was an answer to it, therefore I asked one of our employees here to see if he could find him. He did find him. He asked him to come out in the hall. I told him the accusations which had been made by Mr. Baron. If he wanted to appear and testify under oath, to tell the truth, that he would have an opportunity, and I then came in—and he said he did want to so testify—I came in, and I sent that word to Mr. Teague, and you know what has happened from that point to now.

MR. WYDLER. I do.

MR. TEAGUE. We have 2 minutes left, Mr. Wydler.

MR. WYDLER. Did you ever speak with Mr. Baron about the 012 fire?

MR. HOLMBURG. Casually, yes.

MR. WYDLER. What does that mean, "casually"?

MR. HOLMBURG. He has ideas of what caused the fire. He did most of the talking about it and I listened to speculations on that thing. I never made any comments about what caused it or I never told him exactly what caused it.

I was never near the accident when it happened.

MR. FULTON. Mr. Chairman—

MR. TEAGUE. One question.

MR. FULTON. You are certain at no time you gave any statement that you had knowledge of the cause of the Apollo 204 accident that killed three astronauts, that you at no time said that they were in the capsule for 5 minutes without getting out, nor that there had been 9 minutes' notice of a fire and nothing was done about it?

MR. HOLMBURG. No, sir.

MR. FULTON. You are absolutely sure?

MR. HOLMBURG. Yes, sir.

MR. FULTON. Thank you.

That is all.

MR. TEAGUE. The committee will be adjourned.

MR. WYDLER. I would just like to get straight for the record that I have certain additional witnesses that I would like to see before the committee here. I will take this up at the time that the Chair suggests would be the most convenient time. But, I want to make it clear as we adjourn today that I will make this request sometime either in executive session or public sessions, whichever may turn out to be the best time.

I would like to, however, say that I would like to see one thing, and I think the committee should see it. That is the picture, and I think there are moving pictures of the fire that was simulated of the 012 spacecraft fire. They simulated the fire. NASA did some test somewhere, I would like to see the motion pictures of that fire if there are any motion pictures of that test.

MR. TEAGUE. The committee is adjourned.

MR. DADDARIO. Mr. Chairman, one moment, before you adjourn.

I would like to just say one thing at this time. One matter has stood in my mind since we questioned some of the people at the top of the pad where the tragedy took place. The names of the men I don't recall. But, I am referring to the pad leader and the people with him. I would like to have their names.

(Information requested is as follows:)

D.O. Babbitt, NAA Pad Leader.
J.D. Gleaves, NAA Mechanical Lead Technician.
L.D. Reece, NAA Quality Control.
H.H. Rogers, NASA Quality Control.

Above personnel are those interviewed by the Committee at Complex 34 on the morning of April 21, 1967. For a complete list of those personnel on levels A-7 and A-8 of the Service Structure during the accident, refer to Panel 12 report, pages D-12-7 through D-12-9.

MR. DADDARIO. I believe that under the conditions that they were operating under at the time of the accident—the great heat, flame, and smoke—these men, notwithstanding the finding of the board that there was not adequate fire and rescue teams available at the time, and, acting on their own under extremely dangerous conditions, acted with great courage. I think that we all ought to commend them, and understand that they reacted as competent, experienced and brave men should. We are in their debt for what they tried to do on that day.

MR. TEAGUE. I certainly agree with the gentleman, and the committee is adjourned.

(Whereupon, at 3 p.m., the committee was adjourned.)

COMMENTARY

Baron prepared a 55 page report and a much larger one of some 500 pages. Now, one would think that in a case involving the deaths of three leading astronauts that this report would be available for further study. But six years of effort (non-continuous, of course) had yielded *not a single page!* And this despite queries to NASA, the prime contractor, NAA and even former VP Mondale.

It is obvious that the NASA-NAA conspiracy had been successful in dropping the report into what George Orwell would have termed a "memory hole". As you will recall from his great novel "1984", when the oligarchy found material that was in opposition to their views and edicts, the material simply disappeared.

However, just as the revised edition of this book was going to press, I received copies of the Baron and Philips reports from Senator Alan Cranston of California.

Even the most cursory review of these reports, studied side by side, corroborates the contentions that the moon flights were faked. In point after point, one supports the other. Beginning on the opposite page, pertinent sections of these two reports, along with General Phillips' letter to the president of NAA, are reproduced. Although the material has been re-typed to improve legibility and the author has placed certain key phrases in italics for emphasis, they have not been edited in any other way and their content is identical to that of the originals.

If any two documents lend credibility to the contention that the Apollo flights were faked, they are most certainly the Baron Report and the Phillips Report. They were authored by two men of obvious integrity and dedication. Although from diverse backgrounds, both Tom Baron and Sam Phillips were in total agreement on one basic premise, *i.e.*, that North American Aviation and its sponsor, NASA, were totally unequal to the task of assuring even *one* successful flight to the moon! It becomes obvious that the hidden entities that carried out the hoax took their initial cues from these two reports. And when Grissom, Chaffee and White were burned to death in a command capsule in 1967, the die was cast for all time — a hoax had to be perpetrated or much of value to the establishment would be forever lost . . . mainly their ability to bamboozle the public. As an interesting sidelight to the Phillips report, J. L. Atwood, the president of NAA and to whom it was addressed, initially *denied* having received it! How can anyone ignore a massive documentation totalling 372 pages!

A REPORT BY GENERAL SAMUEL
C. PHILLIPS, MAJOR GENERAL
USAF, APOLLO PROGRAM DIRECTOR
TO J. L. ATWOOD, PRESIDENT
NORTH AMERICAN AVIATION INC.
Dec. 1965

*National Aeronautics
and Space Administration*

WASHINGTON, D.C. 20546

(All italics are by author for emphasis of important points.)

Mr. J. L. Atwood
President
North American Aviation, Inc.
1700 E. Imperial Highway
El Segundo, California

Dear Lee:

I believe that I and the team that worked with me were able to examine the Apollo Spacecraft and S-II stage programs at your Space and Information Systems Division in sufficient detail during our recent visits to formulate a reasonably accurate assessment of the current situation concerning these two programs.

I am definitely *not satisfied* with the progress and outlook of either program and am convinced that the right actions now can result in substantial improvement of position in both programs in the relatively near future.

Inclosed are ten copies of the notes which we compiled on the basis of our visits. They include details not discussed in our briefing and are provided for your consideration and use.

The conclusions expressed in our briefing and notes are critical. Even with due consideration of hopeful signs, *I could not find a substantive basis for confidence in future performance.* I believe that a task group drawn from NAA at large could rather quickly verify the substance of our conclusions, and might be useful to you in setting the course for improvements.

2

MA ltr to   December 19, 1965
J. L. Atwood

    The *gravity of the situation* compels me to ask that
you let me know, by the end of January if possible,
the actions you propose to take. If I can assist in any
way, please let me know.

               Sincerely,

               SAMUEL C. PHILLIPS
               Major General, USAF
               Apollo Program Director

NASA REVIEW TEAM REPORT

I. Introduction

This is a report of the NASA's Management Review of North American Aviation Corporation management of the Saturn II Stage (S-II) and Command Service Module (CSM) programs. The Review was conducted as a result of *the continual failure of NAA to achieve the progress required* to support the objective of the Apollo Program.

The scope of the review included an examination of the Corporate organization and its relationship to and influence on the activities of S&ID, the operating Division charged with the execution of the S-II and CSM programs. The Review also included examination of NAA off-site program activities at KSC and MTF.

The members of the Review Team were specifically chosen for their experience with S&ID and their intimate knowledge of the S-II and CSM programs. The Review findings, therefore, are a culmination of the judgments of responsible government personnel directly involved with these programs. The team report represents an assessment of the contractor's performance and existing affecting current and future progress, and recommends actions believed necessary to achieve an early return to the position supporting Apollo program objectives.

The Review was conducted from November 22 through December 6 and was organized into a Basic Team, responsible for over-all

2.

assessment of the contractor's activities and the relationships
among his organizational elements and functions; and sub-teams
who assessed the contractor's activties in the following areas:

Program Planning and Control (including Logistics)

Contracting, Pricing, Subcontracting, Purchasing

Engineering

Manufacturing

Reliability and Quality Assurance.

Review Team membership is shown in Appendix 7.

Team findings and recommendations were presented to NAA Corporate and S&ID management on December 19.

II. *NAA's Performance to Date - Ability to Meet Commitments.*
At the start of the CSM and S-II Programs, key milestones were
agreed upon, performance requirements established and cost plans
developed. These were essentially commitments made by NAA to
NASA. As the program progressed *NASA has been forced to accept
slippages in key milestone accomplishments, degradation in
hardware performance*, and increasing costs.

A. *S-II*

1. Schedules

As reflected in Appendix VI *key performance milestones*
in testing, *as well as end item hardware deliveries,
have slipped continuously* in spite of deletions of both
hardware and test content. The fact that the delivery

3.

of the common bulkhead test article was rescheduled 5 times, for a total slippage of more than a year, the All System firing rescheduled 5 times for a total slippage of more than a year, and S-II-1 and S-II-2 flight stage of more than a year, are *indicative of NAA's inability to stay within planned schedules*. Although the total Apollo program was reoriented during this time, the S-II flight stages have remained behind schedules even after this reorientation.

2. Costs

The S-II cost picture, as indicated in Appendix VI has been essentially a series of cost escalations with a bow wave of peak costs advancing steadily throughout the program life. Each annual projection has shown either the current or succeeding year to be the peak. NAA's estimate of the total 10 stage program has more than tripled. These increases have occurred despite the fact that there have been reductions in hardware.

3. Technical Performance

The S-II stage is still plagued with technical difficulties as illustrated in Appendix VI. Welding difficulties, insulation bonding, continued redesign as a result of component failures during qualification are indicative of insufficiently aggressive pursuit of technical resolutions during the earlier phases of the program.

4.

B. *CSM*

1. Schedules

    A history of slippages in meeting key CSM milestones
    is contained in Appendix VI. The propulsion spacecraft,
    the systems integration spacecraft, and the spacecraft
    for the first development flight *have each slipped more
    than six months.* In addition, the first manned and the
    *key environmental ground spacecraft have each slipped
    more than a year.* These slippages have occurred in
    spite of the fact that schedule requirements have been
    revised a number of times, and seven articles, originally
    required for delivery by the end of 1965, have been
    eliminated. Activation of two major checkout stations
    was completed more than a year late in one case and more
    than six months late in the other. *The start of major
    testing in the ground test program has slipped from
    three to nine months in less than two years.*

2. Costs

    Analysis of spacecraft forecasted costs as reflected in
    Appendix VI reveals NAA has not been able to forecast
    costs with any reasonable degree of accuracy. The peak
    of the program cost has slipped 18 months in two years.
    In addition, NAA is forecasting that the total cost of
    the reduced spacecraft program will be greater than the
    cost of the previous planned program.

5.

   3. Technical Performance
      Inadequate procedures and controls in bonding and
      welding, as well as inadequate master tooling, have delayed
      fabrication of airframes. In addition, there are still
      major development problems to be resolved. SPS engine
      life, RCS performance, stress corrosion, and failure of
      oxidizer tanks has resulted in degradation of the Block I
      spacecraft as well as forced postponement of the
      resolution of the Block II spacecraft configuration.

III. *NASA Assessment - Probability of NAA Meeting Future Commit-
    ments*
   A. *S-II*
      *Today, after 4½ years and a little more than a year before
      first flight, there are still significant technical problems
      and unknowns affecting the stage.* Manufacture is at least
      5 months behind schedule. NAA's continued inability to meet
      internal objectives, as evidenced by 5 changes in the manufac-
      turing plan in the last 3 motnhs, clearly indicates that
      extraordinary effort will be required if the contractor is
      to hold the current position, let alone better it. The MTF
      activation program is being seriously affected by the insula-
      tion repairs and other work required on the All Systems
      stage. The contractor's most recent schedule reveals further
      slippage in completion of insulation repair. Further,
      integration of manual GSE has recently slipped 3 weeks as

6.

a result of configuration discrepancies discovered during engineering checkout of the system. Failures in timely and complete engineering support, poor workmanship, and other conditions have also contributed to the current S-II situation. Factors which have caused these problems still exist. The two recent funding requirement exercises, with their widely different results, coupled with NAA's demonstrated history of unreliable forecasting, as shown in Appendix VI, leave little basis for confidence in the contractor's ability to accomplish the required work within the funds estimated. *The team did not find significant indications of actions underway to build confidence that future progress will be better than past performance.*

B. *CSM*

With the first unmannned flight spacecraft finally delivered to KSC, there are still significant problems remaining for both Block I and Block II CSM's, *Technical problems with electrical power capacity*(*), service propulsion, structural integrity, weight growth, etc. have yet to be resolved.

Test stand activation and undersupport of GSE still retard scheduled progress. *Delayed and compromised ground and qualification test programs give us serious concern that fully qualified flight vehicles will not be available to support the lunar landing program.* NAA's inability to meet spacecraft contract use deliveries has caused rescheduling of the total

AUTHOR'S NOTE: It was determined that electrical failure caused the fire which killed the three astronauts.

7.

Apollo program. *Appendix VI indicates the contractor's schedule trends which cause NASA to have little confidence that the S&ID will meet its future spacecraft commitments.* While our management review indicated that some progress is being made to improve the CSM outlook, *there is little confidence that NAA will meet its schedule and performance commitments* within the funds available for this portion of the Apollo program.

8.

IV. *Summary Findings*

Presented below is a summary of the team's views on those program conditions and fundamental management deficiencies that are impeding program progress and that require resolution by NAA to ensure that the CSM and S-II Programs regain the required program position. The detail findings and recommendations of the individual sub-team reviews are Appendix to this report.

A. NAA performance on both programs is characterized by *continued failure* to meet committed schedule dates with required technical performance and within costs. *There is no evidence of current improvement in NAA's managament of these programs of the magnitude required to give confidence that NAA performance will improve at the rate required to meet established Apollo program objectives.* *

B. Corporate interest in, and attention to, S&ID performance against the customer's stated requirements on these programs is considered passive. With the exception of the recent General Office survey of selected functional areas of S&ID, *the main area of Corporate level interest appears to be in S&ID's financial outlook* and in their cost estimating and proposal efforts. While we consider it appropriate that the responsibility and authority for execution of NASA programs be vested in the operating Division, this does not relieve the Corporation of its responsibility, and accountability to NASA for results.

One year later, the fatal accident occurred on Pad 34, verifying Gen. Phillips' worst predictions.

AN APOLLO REPORT
by
THOMAS RONALD BARON

AUTHOR'S NOTE: *This report was submitted to a Congressional investigating committee in April 1967, having been compiled the previous year by Baron. He was found dead in his car at a railway crossing only a few days after submitting his report. All italics were added by the author for emphasis of important points.*

AN APOLLO REPORT
by
THOMAS RONALD BARON

PREFACE

It has often been said that "People must do what they think is right". In many cases this has been a costly quotation to follow, but it is probably one of the very few ways we have of advancing ourselves as a nation. There are too many opportunities for organizations to live off of the taxpayer. It always seems that the more tax monies that can be had, the more this money that is wasted. There is no question in my mind that there is gross mismanagement in relation to manhours and proper control of materials, and to the treatment of people. In my opinion, North American Aviation has had the funds to correctly administer a Space Program without compromising the safety of its employees, the astronauts, or the objectives of the Project itself.

North American Aviation, has *not*, in many ways, met their contractual obligations to the United States Government or the taxpayer. I do not have all the information I need to prove all that is in this report. I just hope someone with the proper authority will use this information as a basis to conduct a proper investigation. Someone had to make known to the public and the government what infractions are taking place. I am attempting to do that, someone else will have to try to correct the infractions.

Thomas R. Baron

BRIEF SUMMARY

There are many reasons why this report is being written. I have been with NAA for the past sixteen months. During that time I took the time to make notes on daily happenings. There were difficulties with people, parts, equipment, and procedures. Not to mention, poor safety practices and the accidents they caused. These notes, which were sometimes in the form of letters, were sent up to channels, starting with the leadman. In most cases, as far as I can remember, were not acted upon or never got further than the leadman.

When I was hired by NAA, I was assigned to the Quality Control Department. I was told of the vast importance of my task, and of the great responsibility associated with it. I was told how the slightest infraction could be detrimental to the objectives of the program. I, along with others, was told how important our job was when it came to manned launches. We were told to report every infraction, no matter how minor we felt it was. Unfortunately, this is not practiced by the Company.

The Apollo program is only the beginning, but this is not to be used as an excuse for poor operations. I was just recently told by management that we were still in research and development even if we are going manned. I go along with this for the most part, but we should not compromise the safety of the astronauts just for the benefit of a schedule.

Trying to keep this schedule has cost the taxpayer a great deal of money. Money wasted due to the tremendous waste of manhours, materials, parts, and equipment. The proof of the waste is not too difficult to verify. It would take an investigation of procedures and interviewing several conscientious people. I am not talking about interviewing full supervisors or managers. I'm saying, interview the technicians, the mechanics, the QC man in the area of work. These are the people who know what is really going on as far as wasted manhours and materials, is concerned.

GENERAL NOTES

    The incidents that are described in this report can be put into several categories. I have listed these categories for the benefit and clarification of the reader.

    It must be noted that all of these problems were given to my superiors at the time they took place or shortly thereafter. Many of the problems could and should have been eliminated or prevented if NAA took the proper steps to do so. *Almost every case of trouble gave a clear warning as to what was going to happen.*(*) This is why I say, that if the leadman, or assistant supervisor too the proper action the problem for the most part, could have been avoided.

Lack of coordination between people in responsible positions.

Lack of communication between almost everyone.

The fact that people in responsible positions did not take many of the problems seriously.

Engineers operating equipment instead of technical people.

Many technicians do not know their job. This is partly due to the fact that they are constantly shifted from one job to another.

People are lax when it comes to safety.

People are lax when it comes to maintaining cleanliness levels.

We do not make a large enough effort to enforce the PQCP.

People do not get an official tie-in time period.

We do not maintain proper work and systems records.

---

* *This is a prophetic remark in view of the fact that wiring failures preceded the fatal fire on Pad 34.*

NAA does not give the working force a feeling of accomplishment.

There is not one procedure that I can remember that was completed without a deviation, either written or oral.

Allowing ill practices to continue when the Company is aware of them.

The constant transfer of QC and technical types of people to different types of tasks. Many of the techs will tell the QC man that they have never done that type of job before, or used that type of equipment before. This is one of the most prevalent problems NAA has.

The following is a list of policies that NAA should follow to make themselves the "professional" people they should be in the first place. I am afraid the public had the wrong image in their minds when they think of project Apollo. They probably believe that everyone knows exactly what they are doing at all times. They probably also believe that the work out here at the launch complexes is done on a routine manner. They are wrong. I have been told by two managers that we are still in research and development stages even if we are going to send up a manned spacecraft. This, I firmly believe is the wrong approach to the project. Does NASA know or realize that every spec that we have is inadequate for the task being done? Do they really know that they are changed constantly to comply with the output of quality of the part or system being tested? Are they fully aware of the compromising position that NAA has put the program in? Do they know that of the great number of people we have working on hardware are not satisfied with their own work and the work of others? NASA is not even aware of the vast snags that go on in receiving inspection. Do they really know where all the parts and materials come from? I believe that all these questions can be answered with the word "No".

If an OCP has been written for a specific system, it should not be changed.

Process specifications should not be changed to conform to the results of a test on a component.

Men should be assigned to a specific task or area and stay there. In this way his chances of promotion increase. Too many people get "transferred" just before they get used to a system or work area. If they stayed where they were we would really be building a "professional" group of engineers, technicians and mechanics. As it stands now, we have very few.

Our supervisors or anyone else that writes Internal Letters should coordinate with the people that will be affected by the letter. In most cases this does not appear to be done.

We should completely eliminate all verbal orders.

All launch people, troubleshooting people, systems engineers should work much more closely with NASA. I believe if we had more NASA people to see if the contractor is meeting their contractual obligations many problems could be eliminated. I would think that a project of this magnitude, would warrant this surveillance.

A safety group that would take care of safety infractions immediately.

Schedule shifts so they give a man a firm tie-in time that they get paid for.

Immediately investigate improper practices and don't sluff them off.

Solve their vast problem of communications between all the people.

Many of the problems that are written about, have to do with the morale of the working people. There has been, at different times, a great deal of apathy on the part of these people. Much of this is caused by poor working conditions for they are prevalent in some areas. At pad 34 the bath room facilities are extremely poor. There doesn't seem to be enough trailers available for the working personnel. The technicians at one time had all their tool boxes, extra clothing, etc. in a small semi-truck trailer. The technicians also stayed in this trailer. They had no other place to go. Many times we had to be exposed to the elements for extended periods of time, there were no people to relieve us or no one scheduled a relief. People have missed lunches due to this problem. The anxiety of the Company to protect the men by enforcing the safety policies, is another worry of the men. I remember a man that refused to go into escape operation, because he did not feel safe. He had to report to the assistant QC manager.

The constant transfers of men from one task to another, even if they are in the middle of a test, is distracting to the technician. He never really knows if the test was completed properly or if some problem arose that he could have helped with because he was familiar with the original set-up. He is left without any feeling of accomplishment for the task he started. NAA does not realize that this feeling is important to a good technician or mechanic.

AUTHOR'S NOTE: *Baron's report, written about a year after Phillips', reflects that little if anything was done to remedy Phillips' many complaints.*
It is evident that "business as usual" prevailed and eventually brought about the disaster of January 27, 1967 --- the fire on Pad 34 that claimed the lives of three fine men.

We Never Went To The Moon

TERMINATION

I had an official "OK" to return to work from the Company doctor on the 5th of January.

When I returned to work on the 5th of January, the following events took place.

I walked into my supervisors' office at 1445 hours. Mr. Buffington seemed happy to see me. He immediately took the Doctors' Report from me as I handed it to him, and he said "Let's go upstairs to John's office". (John Hansel, QC Manager) When we arrived upstairs, I was told to wait in John's office for him. Mr. Buffington had gone down the hall. In about twenty minutes John and Don came into the office. I was ushered into the office and sat down at the long table in the office. As soon as I had sat down John said "You've got your car here, drive down to the CAC and I'll meet you there, something about a problem that Labor Relations wants to see you about."

When I arrived at CAC, I went into the Labor Relations office, and said "hello" to Don Ulsh. Another man was there, but I don't recall his name; He was also Labor Relations. Shortly thereafter, John Hansel came into the office and as he did, he closed the door behind him. Don Ulsh spoke first. "I'm sorry, Tom, but I have an unfortunate task to perform." I knew at that time that I was going to be terminated. I immediately told Don, "Don't feel bad, Don, I was expecting this." and added, "It is no surprise to me." I then asked John what some of the reasons were, and he told me the following:

That I was not taking care of my personal financial problems.

AUTHOR'S NOTE: Baron was fired mainly because he revealed what Phillips' report had already verified. But Phillips was promoted up and out of the way while Baron went to meet his death at a railroad crossing. MORAL: Be sure you have at least one star on your collar before you cross swords with the real establishment.

That my ex-wife had contacted him on several occasions.

That I had been served papers at work.

That for the past twelve months, due to my illness, I have only been on the job eight or nine months.

That he did not like the way I had handled this report in reference to newspaper people. He did not think I should have given them the information I had collected.

He felt that I was channeling my efforts in the wrong direction.

I asked him if my work had anything to do with my termination. He stated, that as far as my work was concerned he couldn't ask for a better job.

I was terminated at four o'clock that evening. It was a very sorrowful event for me. There was nothing more that I wanted, than to be associated with the space program.

POOR WORKMANSHIP

Mechanics manufactured a "new" one-quarter inch line. It was being sent through receiving inspection enroute to the Bendix labs for cleaning. The "new" line had a new part number etched on it, but it was of extremely poor quality. It was hardly legible. Unfortunately, this same line also had another part number on it. This part number was hidden with a piece of masking tape. It was neatly wrapped around the area where the number was.

When inspection had asked service engineers to make sure they had the type of system (fuel, oxidizer, oxy) on the Vendors' Instruction Sheet, they would not, for the most part, comply. In one case, when I had asked an engineer about it, he said he was going to mark all the lines and fittings "For GN2 systems". This is one system that doesn't require any special cleaning treatment. (In critical systems, the use of lubricants and the type of system determine what cleaning measures are required.)

A clamp that held an ECS valve in place in the command module was damaged. The engineer straightened out this clamp by hand and wrote "OK AS IS" on the DR. This clamp was a replacement for another clamp that was damaged during packaging or shipment.

People sleeping on the job when they should be watching consoles. This was a constant problem during water glycol testing.

People read magazines, newspapers, etc., when they should be monitoring panels on consoles.

Men coming to work on the pad with alcohol in their system in excessive amounts.

NASA PARTICIPATION IN APOLLO

We definitely need more NASA coverage in all aspects of the program. There are too many times that the authority of a NASA counterpart could have helped the situation.

In receiving inspection there is no NASA. This is to say there is no NASA there to survey the work. I sincerely feel, that if NASA were in the area, many problems could be prevented and others kept from getting larger. We don't have a NASA man in this area to verify any shipments made on second and third shift. This coverage was eliminated by letter.

If more NASA people were on hand in the areas there would be a lesser tendency of NAA techs, engineers, and some QC people to try and "snow" their way through a task.

I have also seen where NASA did not take too much interest in a job. I had occasion just recently in the SITE lab where a NASA man was more interested in his "skin" book than in the test in progress. Then again, I have worked with some that I was proud to be associated with. Men that didn't bend to the point where *they were compromising the safety of the astronauts* or the objective of the Project.

BARON

LIFE SUPPORT OPERATIONS

The following is what I feel is standard operating procedure in the life support area. I base this on the fact that I have witnessed some of the worst performance of technicians and engineers since I have been on this project.

We were in the process of preparing to check out a ECS pressure relief valve for spacecraft 012. We were supposed to use the leak detector in the C14-415. But unfortunately it was not in working order. It seems it hadn't been serviced for some time. There was water in the system, but it was not usable due to the amount of air in the system also. As usual, the second shift engineer picked up the telephone and called his first counterpart, this seemed to be normal procedure for him. The first shift engineer told him to use another gage on the panel. The gage he told him to use was a 0 to 100 pound gage with an accuracy of two percent at full scale. The tolerance of the pressure relief valve leak test was supposed to be a decay rate of no more than two tenths of one pound in fifteen minutes. This leak rate was not possible to see using this gage.

This same valve was supposed to maintain to a level three as far as cleaning was concerned. The interior of the valve had a large amount of a black substance in it. This was later found to be a thread lubricant. The valve was cannibalized from spacecraft 020.

When I suggested another gage be used, a call was made and soon another gage arrived. It was a large Heise gage with a range of zero to one thousand pounds. It was also marked with a red label that said

EDITOR'S NOTE: *Beginning above and continuing for the next few pages, related sections of the earlier Phillips report are interspersed with the Baron report. Baron's work appears first, with the relevant Phillips copy following in italics.*

"RCS SYSTEM ONLY". It was the technician's suggestion to remove the tag, use the gage, and put the tag back on. These kind of people make me sick. We have these kind of people on this program and we don't seem to be able to do much about it.

PHILLIPS

This raises a question as to the effectiveness of the PRIDE program which was designed to motivate personnel toward excellence of performance as a result of a feeling of personal responsibility for the end product.

BARON

LIFE SUPPORT

During the cleaning and assembly of the tank door and the stand-pipe, several operations were noted that jeopardize the integrity of the unit.

No steps in the TPS to tell the technicians how the tank door was to be assembled. This portion of the TPS was supposedly in work at 1500 hours that day. As of 1900 hours that same night, there was no Mos sheet made up.

The stand pipe was assembled without any torque value. The area did not have the proper tools to do the job. (A crow's foot of the proper size was not available, instead they installed it with a large crescent wrench.) The unit was supposedly cleaned to Level Two. This is not possible in a system that has teflon tape in the unit.

Inadequate people to verify the specific clean level.

The unit was improperly packaged. It had an inner sealed bag. The outer bag was intact until a technician stamped the parts tag and clean level tag to it. This is not allowed on this second bag.

The tank door and pipe assembly was not packaged properly for delivery to the s/c. It had no other covering aside from the afore-mentioned bags. It was then carried into a carryall by two men. It naturally did not fit into the carryall completely. The pipe assembly was fourteen feet long so I would say that at least five feet of it was hanging outside the rear of the carryall. At this time it was still being held by the two technicians. This complete procedure is against trans-porting and cleaning specs. If I would have made any attempt to stop the people and hold up the test I would have had the night supervisor on my neck again. Why all this goes on, and *why the people higher up don't realize the risk involved in some of these ill practices, I'll never know.* (*)

TIME - November 1966

Record keeping in this area is very poor. There is one desk in the area that is used as a "filing cabinet" for many different records. Some of the records are just lying around in the different drawers at random. Some of these records include the following:

Cleanliness records of all the different facility gases used.

Cleanliness records of all the different facility liquids used.

Cleanliness records of the different rooms in the building.

AUTHOR'S NOTE: Again, the Phillips report was undoubtedly suppressed since even an aware person like Baron did not know it existed. If he had, he would have related it to his own report.

Cleanliness records of the different gases in the check-out units.

Records of the different units that have had a preinstallation test.

Many TAIR books that are of the soft cover type.

There is also a duplication of "official" records being kept in this area. Much confusion can result from this if it is not taken care of now.

Normally, when a component must be tested. an engineer will write a TPS. He then should notify the area inspector that a TPS has been written. The inspector, in turn, logs this TPS in the Space Craft Spares TAIR book. Unfortunately, this book is about a mile down the road. It is kept in receiving inspection area at the warehouse. The inspector seldom calls anyone at receiving inspection to log the TPS into the book. It is usually done after the TPS is complete. This is a complete reversal of normal procedure. A TAIR book is also kept in the life support area but it is not an "official" book. The book in the life support area gets all the required stamps and the book that should have them is in receiving. If this sounds confusing to read, imagine how difficult it is to work with.

I was told when I went to work in this building that I was not to create "waves" and above all, don't stop any tests, no matter what. This was said to me by my assistant supervisor, Dick Shrieves.

PHILLIPS

It is not NASA's intent to dictate solutions to the deficiencies noted in this report. The solution to NAA's internal problems is both a prerogative and a responsibility of NAA Management, within the parameters of NASA's requirements as stated in the contracts. NASA does, however, fully expect objective, responsible, and timely action by NAA to correct the conditions described in this report.

BARON

QUADS

SPACECRAFT 011

Engineer John Tribe operated almost all of the test equipment by himself.

Engineering did not wait for QC inspector to verify many steps.

Tolerances were deviated from constantly.

Almost a total lack of safety procedures during testing.

Technicians, who were very capable, could not operate the equipment. They had to stand around in the area.

One copy of the test procedure was used for four separate Quads. This made it very difficult to follow the test proceedings.

Very poor workmanship on splicing of instrumentation on the Quads.

Quads transferred to different areas without proper paperwork.

Flagrant violations of cleanliness of the Quads.

Splices were not the proper size (instrumentation).

One quad was left in the middle of the MSOB floor. There was work done on the day shift which resulted in metal shavings, filings, etc., by another contractor. The work was done approximately fifteen feet away from the quad. Metal shavings and dust from a drill press was on the work bench.

Still another quad was found in the MSOB hi-bay area totally un-covered. Length of time it was uncovered was not determined.

Some quads were received in such poor condition, they had to be sent immediately back to Downey, California.

PHILLIPS

The condition of hardware shipped from the factory, with thousands of hours of work to complete, is unsatisfactory to NASA. S&ID must complete all hardware at the factory and further implement, without delay, an accurate system to certify configuration of delivered hardware, properly related to the DD 250.

BARON

QUADS

4-11-66 QA. MSOB. Hi-Bay   Typical Day of Quad Work

Subject Quads

As usual the confusion here is no less than anywhere else. The situation looks almost hopeless. Parts are not here, work being accomplished wrong has been redone. Cleanliness specs are not being abided by. *We will end up in deep trouble.*

Why can't we have organization and the type of supervision we need, the lack of even the most inexpensive tool is one major problem and it is ridiculous. Crimping extraction tools and the similar types of tools, the lack of co-ordination.

QA.4-14-66 MSOB "B"OCP K4072

1. Put shortage sheets in QD-A Book.

2. Pick up dates stamp.

3. Calibrate equipment up to date.

4. Check B/O Box for propriety.

5. Pick up on page No. 60 of K4072.

6. Extreme noise in area, jack hammer being used approx. 150'
   away and below this 28' level.

7. Bought off TPS, 003 and MOD No. 1 on Quad C.

8. Oxidizer blanket sensor wires removed from TB4 without auth.

9. 15 of the blanket latches have the safety wires removed.

PHILLIPS

i. Quality

*NAA quality is not up to NASA requirements. This is evidenced
by the large number of "correction" E.O.'s and manufacturing
discrepancies that escape NAA inspectors but are detected by
NASA inspectors. NAA must take immediate and effective
action to improve the quality of workmanship and to tighten their
own inspection. Performance goals for demonstrating high quality
must be established, and trend data must be maintained and given
serious attention by Management to correct this unsatisfactory
condition.*

BARON

WATER GLYCOL

Jan. 6, 1966

Conditions of system at this time:

This was the third attempt to complete this test.

Number one pump was not working properly.

Number two pump was burnt up at 1740 hours.

Back-up system was in repair.

We still had the leaking QD on the NASA interface panel.

Flowmeter did not have a completed calibration.

No QC coverage in some areas.

It appeared today that the engineers on the system were getting apathetic about their work. They did not seem to be too alarmed or concerned over the situation. The lack of going by procedure was evident. Perhaps with all the difficulty we were having, going by any kind of procedure was out of the question. It would have been wise at this time to shut down the entire operation and repair the entire system, and then try to run the test as it should be run.

PHILLIPS

Summary:

Effective planning and control from a program standpoint does not exist. Each organization defines its own job, its own schedules, and its own budget, either of which may or may not be compatible or developed in a manner required to achieve program objectives. For example, schedules — end-item delivery requirements are defined by contract and reflected in Program Master Development Schedules prepared by the Program Manager's Office. In the initial planning cycle, each organization blocks out a peroiod of time required to do its job. This is up to the interface with engineering. Engineering determines when it can release the technical data which, in most cases, undersupports the using organization's requirements. Thus, material and manufacturing flow times are reduced. This is not necessarily wrong. However, nothing is done to ensure that engineering will meet uts committed release dates.

AUTHOR'S NOTE: Rather than belabor the issue, it is sufficient to conclude this comparison of BARON and PHILLIPS in their respective reports. Many hundreds of comparisons could be made but I believe that our point is made by the foregoing examples. Both Tom Baron and Sam Phillips knew that Apollo was on the rocks technologically. And while this information was generally suppressed in the media, it did not escape the attention of those who make high-level decisions. Thus, following the fire on Pad 34, there was never any doubt that the moon landings would be simulated since reaching the moon with a hodge-podge of malfunctioning hardware was an obvious impossibility!

AUTHOR'S NOTE: *The fatal fire on Pad 34 was the turning point of the entire Apollo project. Phillips' warnings and counsel had been ignored along with Baron's. NAA went carelessly on as the following references by Baron to Pad 34 indicate. At this time, Grissom began to voice unauthorized comments regarding the Apollo project and it is the author's firm belief that he was silenced as an example to the other astronauts. Yes, I am charging murder, and if not by intent then certainly by gross negligence as, again, the following data proves. In short, it was murder either way you approach it.*

I refer the reader to the section on the Congresssional investigation wherein Baron states that the astronauts attempted to get out of the command module before the fire started. Now, the reader is asked to consider that fact in view of what has just been presented . . . a tale of mismanagement, ineptitude, rampant negligence and terminal apathy. The astronauts must have known about the sorry condition of Apollo and thus it is not surprising that they wanted OUT at the first sign of danger. During the time that the author was employed by Rocketdyne, a part of his assignment was to aid in the writing of procedure manuals for tank entry and safety. It was always heavily stressed that no one should enter a confined space without easy egress and some means of life support should conditions turn lethal. It is curious that this procedure did not apply to such an obviously dangerous "tank" as the command capsule.

PAD 34

Removal of cables without authorization.

When the totalizer did not work on the 002 unit, the troubleshooting that took place was a farce. 12-7-65.

Some of the DTT boxes we used did not have proper identification. Some of the part numbers were not really known.

QC people operated many of the units on the pad during the fueling and launch operations. Some techs were unfamiliar with the equipment.

It is difficult to verify whether or not all the meters, etc., are calibrated.

Safety infractions are listed in another section of this report.

Lack of mechanics to maintain cleanliness on flex lines.

NAA has to borrow tools from other contractors to get the job done.

Circuit breaker kept blowing on the N204 transfer unit. For as long as I can remember this breaker kept blowing and was just reset. I don't know if it has been repaired as of this date.

Headsets were a tremendous problem. People was stashing them, stealing them, etc.

Many times the QC had to give his headset up to a tech so the tech could do a task. This prevented the QC man to know what was going on with the test.

One QC man had to cover as much as four or five jobs at one time.

Lack of scape suits for all people in a test. On space craft nine, I remember when one group of people lived in their scape suits for three or four days, during this time another group of workers played cards, slept., etc., for the same period of time. The reason was that there were no scape suits available for them to wear. We were working twelve hours on and twelve hours off. The waste of money was tremendous. Sometimes we the second shift did not have suits until late at night, and everyone goofed off until we received them.

Communications during scape was terrible. Many times the trailer could not be raised on the headset. This created a lack of confidence with the people in scape on the gantry. Sometimes the scape trailer did not know who was on the pad.

The practice of straightening bent pins in various connectors became common practice.

Work was generally poorly coordinated at the pad. Much time was lost in waiting around for parts or equipment.

Identification of lines is very poor. Fuel and oxidizer lines were not marked as such. It was easy to confuse the parts.

There were times when we had so many techs around they couldn't find a place to hide.

A PCM unit was found on the 200 foot level of the umbilical tower exposed to the elements. It had been raining. I told the proper people and also covered the item. The next day it was still there, uncovered. The PCM unit is a costly item.

The common problem of seals being broken on patch panel, etc., existed at this pad also.

Hardware found laying around loose in these patch boxes. Terminal boards found loose.

Often these boxes were found open and unsealed.

SAFETY INFRACTIONS

Immediately after disconnecting an N_2O_4 line flex located on the seventh level of the gantry at pad 34, a technician walked about fifteen feet away and lit a cigarette. The line had liquid in it and the tech was wearing a splash suit.

The only safety manual we use is an Air Force manual, and many of the regulations are difficult to apply to the space industry.

During a fueling operation on pad 34, the following incident took place. We were in SCAPE at the time and we were in "hot" flow. On one quarter of the pad we had an oxidizer transfer unit. Approximately one hundred or so feet away was the UDMH transfer unit. Between these was a diesel power unit, with a goodly amount of sparks emmiting from its exhaust stack. This was reported by the QC man on the pad. The unit was allowed to continue in operation. It was a night shift operation and the unit was supplying light. Later in the evening, a diesel fuel truck was sent on the pad between the oxidizer transfer unit and the power unit. It proceeded to fuel the power unit. Needless to say it did not put the people working in the immediate area in a safe position. They called it in to the test conductor, but the diesel fueling continued.

The drains around pad 34 are always a hazard to the people working there. Many, many times the top grating of these drains are removed and left open. No warning sign is ever erected. It is extremely difficult to see these openings at night until you are right on top of them. The pits also have stub-ups protruding from them. I believe there is an accident on record where a man had fallen into one of these pits and was injured by a stub-up. Driving in the area is also very dangerous due to these open pits.

Technician using a cigarette lighter so he can read the meters on the panel. This is at the base of the umbilical tower. I reported this to my leadman and absolutely no action was taken.

No net was used for many weeks to safeguard the men on the different levels of the gantry. No chain rails were used either. A man could very easily have fallen through the center hole in the gantry if he wasn't extremely careful.

Relieving of high pressure valves without warning on the gantry. Popping open a 4,000 pound valve is like a small explosion.

As many as three elevators have been out of commission at one time on the gantry. This was very crucial during a scape operation.

Elevators were in extremely poor condition. In some the entire ceiling was rusted out. The corners of the floor was also rusted through.

The room to the elevator motors were kept locked. *One morning about 1:00 A.M. a fire had started in the room.* I could not get into it to even see what was burning. We had to get the contractor people from another pad to gain entrance to the room. There were no maintenance people on the pad during this shift.

We Never Went To The Moon

AUTHOR'S REPRISE, SUMMARY AND CONCLUSIONS

You have just read some amazing documents, heretofore unobtainable. Again, we thank Senator Cranston and his staff for the most timely procurement of both General Phillips' and Tom Baron's reports. The reports are, of course, much longer and more detailed than the brief segments included here. But the samples are clearly representative of the whole. They describe a "chamber of horrors" in existence in the Mid 1960's throughout the entire Apollo program. Nothing worked as planned and the program was slipping badly. Then on top of that miserable situation, the fire of January 27, 1967, put the entire program back at least a year. Thus, at the beginning of 1968, a scant 18 months before the alleged first landing on the moon, the entire Apollo project was no further ahead than it had been at the time when Phillips wrote his damning report to Atwood.

I can make no other conclusion than to believe that efforts were concentrated on the facade of Apollo, the launch and touchdown, with all other efforts scrapped and for good reasons. There was simply no more time to waste trying to squeeze engineering expertise out of an obviously incompetent organization, NAA. Thus, the simulators took over the project and did the best they could. They presented lots of well-faked photographs, laboratory rocks and programmed astronauts. With the help of father-figure Cronkite as the journalistic goat, the sheep-like public was led to believe that we actually landed men on the moon.

But ask yourself this one question . . . can you really, truly and honestly believe that an organization as described by an Air Force general and a poor but competent and dedicated inspector, could perform all of the engineering feats involved in successfully landing 12 men on the moon six times?

The prosecution rests its case on the evidence acquired to date. But the investigation will continue. Thus, readers are welcome to contribute any relevant data, no matter how seemingly insignificant. After all, we are involved in putting together a giant jigsaw puzzle and even the smallest pieces will contribute to the big picture. Write the author c/o DESERT PUBLICATIONS, Cornville, AZ 86325.

Thank you.

We Never Went To The Moon

During Baron's testimony, Mervin Holmburg mysteriously appears in the room at the behest of Robert Smart, an assistant to the president of North American Aviation. He then proceeds to do a hatchet job on Baron. It is possible that Holmburg was even more knowledgeable about the Pad 34 fire but was silenced by a threat of death, the fate suffered by Baron just *four days* after he testified. Holmburg made the astounding revelation to Baron that the astronauts tried to get out of the capsule for FIVE MINUTES without success. Also that the fire had been reported nine minutes before any action was taken.

Consider this scenario. Apollo has been faltering badly. General Samuel Phillips, the Air Force honcho of the project has sent Atwood, the president of NAA, a report very similar in content to Baron's report. (At first Atwood denied receiving it but later recanted). Virgil Ivan "Gus" Grissom has been developing his own report which was taken from him home after his death, read murder. Grissom has also been giving unauthorized interviews to the press regarding his disapproval of the way Apollo is progressing. He even goes so far as to hang a lemon on a command module! The DIA realizes that this situation could become highly critical in a short time . . . a leading and well-liked astronaut blows the whistle on a 30 billion dollar project! Perhaps, thinks the DIA, an accident can be arranged. Something plausible and believable and unsuspected (like Dealey Plaza). So with 100 percent oxygen in the capsule to ensure total burnout, a squib is triggered from the control center. The fire starts and the astronauts seek frantically to exit. But someone has taken care of that . . . the hatch is sealed from the OUTSIDE! Chaffee and White also die in the fire but that's the breaks, according to DIA's reasoning. Two additional lives vs 30 billion dollars is no contest. As George Jackson once said. "the Man is merciless."

The above scenario gains great credibility when you relate it to Holmburg's later-retracted statement. Holmburg inadvertently let the cat out of the bag in talking with Baron. When he realized that he was dealing with people who play for keeps, he began talking with forked tongue. For example, he trips himself up during the questioning by Daddario and Wydler. He first states that he "came of his own free will." Then he says, "well, I work right outside the door and it is my time to come to work now." But a few seconds later, the *real* reason emerges in the person of Robert Smart who states that "he asked an employee to see if he could find him"!!!

In summary, what we see in this interrogation is an attempt to discredit Baron. Even Hechler takes a pot shot at Baron nit-picking regarding the spelling of Slayton's name. Little is reported directly from Baron's two reports and the reports themselves are *not* made a part of the committee's report.

But discrediting was not enough. Baron and his two reports were still a great threat to the coverup. Eliminating the reports is no great problem; DIA agents obtain all copies and they are dropped into a memory hole. Until Senator Cranston's office was able to locate a copy, it was thought highly possible that NO copies existed anywhere! Baron himself is a trifle more troublesome. A friend of mine volunteered the following scenario since he has had direct experience with defectors from the CIA's Air America. Baron and his wife are drugged. His wife is also sacrificed to make the story more credible to the public. They are placed in their car and taken to a railway crossing. The train does the rest.

Despite Florida law which states that accidental death victims must be routinely autopsied, the Barons are cremated and THAT IS THAT! With the reports gone and Baron out of the way, the Apollo hoax can be continued without the presence of an annoying gadfly, a man who put truth before his personal safety. May God rest Baron's brave soul.

In closing, keep in mind that Baron died in an "accident" just a few days after testifying about his report before Congress, Phillips has gone on to promotions into higher, more secretive government bureaucracies — his reward for not pursuing his own revelations? We wonder.

There is a third man present if only by remembrance: Virgil Ivan Grissom. He too authored reports about the poor quality of technology and engineering created by North American Aviation. Some of them were quite graphic, such as hanging a lemon on a command capsule. Unfortunately, his written reports seem to have totally disappeared. They were seized from his home after his death and never returned.

But just as the Baron and Phillips reports suddenly materialized as this book was being completed, perhaps with some renewed energy and effort, the Grissom report will surface also. If so, it will be a major chapter in a future revised edition of this book.

"Murder, though it hath no tongue will speak."
— William Shakespeare

AUTHOR'S NOTE: Both the Baron and Phillips reports are available to readers who wish to examine them in detail. Contact the author c/o DESERT PUBLICATIONS, Cornville, AZ 86325. Eventually, they may be published if sufficient interest is shown in them.

10

Were The Astronauts
Manchurian Candidates?

"There was a lack of reality about everything, a kind of
euphoric strangeness to all was going on."

—Colonel Aldrin

Following his return to earth, Buzz Aldrin experienced an
increasingly severe mental illness. A sampling of quotes from
his revealing book, RETURN TO EARTH, provides a basis
for analysis.

P 22   "This kind of tension simmered for the next few
         weeks but never surfaced."

P 25   "We were to become public relations men for space
         exploration—in a sense, salesmen. The word made
         me terribly uncomfortable and self-conscious when
         it was first used."

P 66   " . . . and a surprise. The people who lined the
         streets were exceedingly polite but not at all en-
         thusiastic." (On his reception in Sweden.)

P 68   "I felt all six of us were fakes and fools for allowing
         ourselves to be convinced by some strange concept
         of duty to be sent . . .

P 288   "My intellect was not separated by the jagged and
         dangerous wall of my emotions. The rule of my

emotions was absolute and ruthless. I yearned for a brightly lit oblivion—wept for it.

P 295 "Should anyone discover I was in the hospital (for nervous problems) the explanation was to be that I was being treated for a neck problem. The other problem, if at all possible, was to be kept secret."

P 304 The last two years of my life, from the time I left the lunar quarantine quarters until I entered Wilford Hall (the mental hospital) were characterized by depression, which occasionally deepened, then rose to a temporary brief high of optimism, only to sink again to a new low."

P 317 "My life is unreal . . ."

P 320 "I was incredulous . . . she had really believed all that crap she had read about me—about her—about all of us? Suddenly, all my life . . . became tinged with a crazy unreality."

P 388 "When I began this book I had two intentions. I wanted it to be as honest as possible."

(Why not just plain honest?)

In June of 1971, Aldrin rejoined the Air Force and was assigned to the Edwards Air Force Base in California, a windy, high desert locale. He had been on medication for his nervous disorder: one Ritalin pill per day. In his own words . . .

"I looked great. There was only one problem. I believed my confidence to be rooted in reality.

"Early in June an event was scheduled that we regarded as a new beginning for us and as such, we looked forward to it a great deal. I wanted to be at my very best.

We Never Went To The Moon

"The occasion was a big meeting of the Lancaster Chamber of Commerce. They had invited members of the Society of Test Pilots; I was one of the guest speakers.

"What intrigued me most was that I would not be giving a speech. Instead, Roy Neal, the NBC newscaster, would interview me in a most informal way.

"The afternoon of the banquet, I stopped by Roy's motel and asked if he wanted to run over any questions with me. He assured me they would be very easy to answer and that no preparation at all was necessary.

"As banquets go, this was a large one. The base commander, General and Mrs. White attended.

"I began to be more and more apprehensive as the time for my interview grew near.

"The first question that Roy Neal asked me was, "Now that almost two years have gone by, why not tell us how it really felt to be on the moon?"

"If any one question was anathema to me, that was it. Roy, I suppose, felt he had no choice. Yet it has always been almost impossible for me to answer that question with any sort of decent response.
"My throat went dry and I became dizzy. Carefully I picked my way through a reply, thinking that all the test pilots in the audience would burst out in laughter.

"I remember little more of the interview. When it was over I stepped down and stood before about 50 Chamber of Commerce members and their wives all waiting for autographs. I signed a few and when the shaking became uncontrollable, I grabbed Joan and ran for the door.

"In the privacy of an alley near the auditorium, I choked back my emotions and quietly wept. Joan stood silently by and when I composed myself, she took me to the nearest bar. I was inconsolable . . . I was judging myself too harshly . . . I got rather drunk."

Commentary

In Hamlet, the hero plans to trap the supposed murderer of his father by staging a play. He says, "The play's the thing wherein I'll catch the conscience of the king." Later, he says, "If he but blench, I'll know my course."

I once discussed the Aldrin incident and its parallel to Shakespeare's play with a specialist in human communication. He said that probably Aldrin's hypnotic state (imposed as a part of the moon trip simulation) was finally terminated by that one critical question asked at a crucial time. ("If he but blench . . .".) Knowing that he had to lie (and a West Point graduate almost never lies) caused the extreme stress which triggered the severe nervous collapse.

If you, the reader of this book, have accomplished some major feat, are you not willing to discuss it? Let's say that you are the first person to have climbed a specific mountain or set a speed record on two wheels. Wouldn't it be a lifelong pleasure to tell people about it IN DETAIL? Aldrin and Armstrong are allegedly the first two human beings to set foot on the moon; certainly that is a major feat assuming it did happen. Then why do both men shun the public eye like the plague? Aldrin has had severe mental problems culminating with acute alcoholism while Armstrong has become reclusive. Why have these personality changes taken place? Before the alleged flight, they were both judged to be as fit, mentally and physically as anyone on earth. This was necessary because of the high-stress activity that they would be called upon to withstand. Why, if the moon landings actually took place, would both men exhibit all the characteristics of persons suffering from guilt?

The most severe pressure was placed on Aldrin and Armstrong since they were the first to perpetrate the hoax. Later, when the public was placed under NASA ether, the other astronauts were able to cope with greater assurance. However, even these men are wary. During the tenth anniversary of Apollo 11, the astronauts gathered in Las Vegas, Nevada. Here, an attempt was made to interview them but with no success. Robert Stoldal, News Director of Channel 8, CBS TV, in Vegas states that none of the astronauts would discuss any aspect of their alleged moon flights. Perhaps they fear that the new technique of psychological stress evaluation will reveal the truth! As you may have learned, President Carter was caught in a number of lies when his speeches were analyzed by PSE.

Fortunately, there are tapes of previous statements by all astronauts and it is the intent of this investigator to have them analyzed as soon as possible. The results will be reported in the next edition of this book. If you can't wait, then do it yourself. Simply get tape or disc recordings made by the astronauts and find someone who has PSE equipment. Your findings will be much appreciated by the author and publisher.

Recently, two major corporations have found themselves in big trouble. Chrysler went blithely on building oversize cars when the public had long since decided to go small. McDonnell-Douglas built a flying turkey called the DC-10 which has the regretable characteristics of coming apart while in flight.

Advertising campaigns for Chrysler featured a sad-faced Armstrong looking most uncomfortable standing by the unsalable cars. And in full page ads touting the reliability of the DC-10, Pete Conrad proclaims that it was the same technology that put him on the moon that was responsible for the "integrity" of the DC-10. (The wry question arises - does Armstrong drive a Chrysler product; does Conrad fly in DC-10's?)

Having public figures act as touts for government hoaxes and scams is common in America. Eisenhower was the patsy for the U-2 fiasco while the current president is firmly ensconced in the pocket of the multi-national oil cartel.

"Murder, tho it hath no tongue, will speak, with most miraculous organ."

Time is on the side of truth as is high technology. Astronauts, we are patient.

11

Common Sense Considerations

There is an old Greek saying from the 1st century BC. "False in part, false in the whole."

In examining the Apollo project from a simplistic, common sense view, we find that many "parts" simply do not make sense. And thus, if any one of the "parts" is false, then we must conclude with the Greeks, that the *whole project* was spurious. Here are a few for your review.

THE LUNAR LANDER

Sometimes called the LM (lunar module) or LEM (lunar excursion module), this ungainly, four-legged device defies all reasonable credibility. Top-heavy and thus unstable, the LM had to lose all lateral motion to avoid tipping over on landing. And yet, in Apollo II, there was continual sidewise motion. If the LM tipped over, there would have been no way for the astronauts to right it. Would any reasonable person count on its stability?

How were the astronauts able to maneuver this steel giraffe successfully the first time? It did not function on earth; Armstrong was nearly killed in the Texas simulator. Again, would a reasonable person expect an untried device to work THE FIRST TIME without prior practice or proof that it WOULD work?

Now if it was able to perform so successfully on the moon, why not use the same device on earth? Why bother with parachutes and ocean landings when one could easily come down on four legs on a celestial body having no atmosphere. The Russians claim soft earth landings and they didn't even try for the moon as it later turned out. Again, if it was so easy to make perfect landings the *first time* without any prior experience, why not use that expertise to land on the White House lawn in the Command Capsule?

We are supposed to believe that the LM touched down safely without any incident six times (Apollo 11 thru 17 sans the scratched 13 trip). Now certainly, the veterans of the early flights would have given their knowledge to those who flew later. But what happens when they tie the Lunar Rover to the side of the LM? Doesn't this change the landing characteristics rather significantly? Even tho it only weighs a few hundred pounds on the moon, it would still affect the handling characteristics of the LM to a marked degree. Anyone who has flown a plane knows how important it is to take into account the loading of cargo especially for landings in touchy situations.

Also, why ship the rover to the moon *three times* when the space and weight could have been used for a telescope to observe the universe. Just imagine what tremendous photos could have been taken of Saturn's rings, the red spot of Jupiter and the Milky Way!

The LM employed a hypergolic *engine which burned hydrazine and nitrogen tetroxide. While it is true that it worked well on earth, there is no assurance that it would perform in the adverse environment of the lunar surface. Here, temperatures vary between plus 250 F and minus 275 F. Valves, pressure regulators, sensors are all prone to failure when confronted with extreme variables. We are asked to believe that this engine, never tried before on the lunar surface, worked flawlessly six times. Having spent many years at Rocketdyne watching engines blow up on the test stands, makes this writer extremely doubtful.

In films of Apollo 14, the trip allegedly made to the Fra Mauro area, the astronauts placed a TV camera so that the liftoff could be televised. Repeated study of the films shows the ascent stage popping up from the descent stage like a cork from a champagne bottle! Furthermore, there is no

* Self-igniting

visible flame!! It is difficult to explain the disbelief that arises from viewing this sequence so the reader is counseled to obtain the footage from the nearest NASA outlet and see for himself.

Incidentally, one former NASA executive commented that while viewing one of the later ascents, a shadow appeared and the TV image was cut off. Inquiries produced the threat of termination.

NASA issued a film in the mid-sixties that showed the entire Apollo effort in animation. The LM descended to the moon's surface spitting flame and digging an enormous crater beneath the engine. In fact, the final scene showed the LM's legs sitting on the edge of the crater. Now the artist's conception had to be based on the technical data then extant which included Surveyor information on the soil characteristics of the lunar surface. Why then, is there not the least trace of soil disturbance beneath ANY of the LM's? Anyone who has witnessed an actual rocket engine firing knows the tremendous power of the flame jet. Furthermore, the flame temperature is close to 5,000 F capable of melting particulate matter in seconds.

We are asked to believe that the LM, weighing about the same as a large American car, descended to the moon's surface with landing engine blasting out 30,000 pounds of thrust and all that happened was that a few "unassociated particles" scurried away from the scene. In actuality, the blast of the descent engine, straining to support the ton and a half structure, would have scoured the landing area to bed rock or at the least, to a significant depth. Discoloration would have also taken place along with fracture of the super-cooled rocks hit by the searing flame.

THE PATTERN OF FAILURE

There are a number of laws that apply to this part of the universe.
"Nature sides with the hidden flaw."
"If a thing can go wrong, it will, at the worst possible moment."

Things mechanical, particularly those of great complexity in a harsh environment, often fail. Take a look at this random sampling of pre-Apollo space ventures: (All are from a NASA Index)

NAME	LAUNCH	VEHICLE	MISSION/REMARKS
GEMINI IX-A	June 3, 1966 June 1, 1966	Titan II . . . . Atlas	Manned: Thomas P. Stafford and Eugene A. Cernan; 44 revolutions; 72 hrs. 21 min. Unable to dock with ATDA (backup for Gemini Target Vehicle) when shroud failed to clear docking adapter 2 hrs. 2 min of EVA accomplished; use of Astronaut Maneuvering Unit prevented by difficulty of donning unit and fogging of spacesuit faceplate.
APOLLO SATURN	July 5, 1966	Uprated Saturn . . . . (SA-203)	Launch Vehicle Development: Liquid hydrogen evaluation flight of the S-IV-B stage vent and restart capability. Also test of S-IV-B/IU separation and cryogenic storage at zero "G". Flight terminated during liquid hydrogen pressure and structural test.
GEMINI X	July 18, 1966 July 18, 1966	Titan II . . . . Atlas Agena	Manned: John W. Young and Michael Collins; 43 rev; 70 hrs., 47 mins. First dual rendezvous (with GTV 10 then with GTV 8); first docked vehicle maneuvers; 3 hatch openings; stand up EVA - 45 mins, terminated due to fumes; umbilical EVA - 27 mins, terminated to conserve maneuvering propellant on S/C; equipment jettisoned before reentry. Micrometeoriod experiment retrieved from GTV-8.
SURVEYOR II	Sept. 20, 1966	Atlas-Centaur . . . . . . (AC-7)	Lunar Exploration: During midcourse maneuver one of the three spacecraft's vernier engines did not ignite causing incorrectable tumbling. Contact lost 5 1/2 hours prior to predicted impact time.
INTELSAT II (HS-303A) NON-NASA Mission	Oct. 26, 1966	Delta (DSV-3E)	Communications: Second ComSat Corp. commercial satellite, NASA providing reimbursable launch support. Apogee motor nozzle blown off shortly after motor ignited. Planned geostationary orbit not achieved; Spacecraft orbit allows about 8 hrs. of use per day.
GEMINI XII	Nov. 11, 1966 Nov. 11, 1966	Titan II . . . . Atlas-Agena	Manned: James A. Lovell, Jr. and Edwin E. Aldrin, Jr.; 59 revs; 94 hrs. 34 min. Final mission of Gemini series emphasized evaluation of EVA (Aldrin: 5 hrs. 37 min.) tasks workload including two "standups" totaling 208 min. and 129 min. of umbilical EVA. Also 14 scientific experiments performed and solar eclipse pictures taken. The target vehicles primary propulsion not usable for high elliptical orbit maneuver.
BIOSATELLITE I	Dec. 14, 1966	Delta (DSV-3G)	Biology: Spacecraft completed three days of operation with good environmental control and attitude control. All biological experiment events occurred. The radiation source functioned as planned. Retro-fire did not occur and recovery was not possible. Spacecraft reentered but was not recovered.

We Never Went To The Moon

NAME	LAUNCH	VEHICLE	MISSION/REMARKS
INTELSAT II-B (HS-303A) NON-NASA Mission	**1967** Jan. 11, 1967	Delta (DSV-3E)	Communications: Third ComSat commercial satellite; NASA providing reimbursable launch support. Capable of handling T.V, data transmission or up to 240 voice channels; part of capacity to be purchased by NASA for Apollo support. Retromotor fired Jan. 14 to place spacecraft in geostationary orbit about 176° East in the vicinity of the Marshall Islands. One of four traveling wave tubes failed.
ESSA IV (TOS-B)	Jan. 26, 1967	Delta (DSV-3E)	Meteorology: Advanced version of cartwheel configuration. Nearly polar sun synchronous orbit. Good APT pictures returned on Jan. 28. January 29 shutter problem made one (of two redundant) APT cameras aboard inoperative.
APOLLO/SATURN 204			Spacecraft fire at Complex 34, Jan. 27, 1967. Astronauts Grissom, White, and Chaffee died.
LUNAR ORBITER III	Feb. 5, 1967	Atlas-Agena	Lunar Photography: 211 set (frames) of medium and high resolution pictures taken. Last frame not taken to cut biomat early. Picture readout terminated by a transient signal which ended film movement. 72% of photos readout. Readout completed for six primary sites, parts of six other sites. Partial readout returned on 31 secondary sites.
ESRO II-A NON-NASA Mission	May 29, 1967	Scout	Solar Astronomy and Cosmic Rays: All telemetry lost eight seconds prior to third stage cut-off. No fourth stage burn, Satellite landed in South Pacific.
SURVEYOR IV	July 14, 1967	Atlas-Centaur	Lunar Exploration: All launch vehicle and spacecraft performance nominal until last two seconds of 42 second retro burn when all communications were lost with spacecraft. Target site: Sinus Medii.
SURVEYOR III (SURVEYOR C)	April 17, 1967	Atlas-Centaur	Lunar Exploration: Achieved soft landing on April 19. Closed loop radar failed during landing and spacecraft landed three times on inertial guidance before its verniers cut off. Surface Sampler experiment discovered pebbles at six inches and 10 psi bearing strength. The spacecraft returned 6,315 pictures.
APOLLO VI (AS-502/CSM-020)	April 4, 1968	Saturn V	Launch Vehicle Development Mission: Anomalies experienced with J-2 engine augmented spark ignitors on second and third stages. S-IVB restart not accomplished. F-1 engines on first stage synchronized creating longitudinal vibration of unacceptable amount. Spacecraft performance nominal.
REENTRY F	April 27, 1968	Scout	Reentry Heating Test Designed to support the advancement of atmospheric entry technology. Spacecraft performance nominal.
NIMBUS B	May 18, 1968	TAT	Meteorology: Carried two experiments on Nimbus II and five new ones. Planned 600 NM sun synchronous circular polar orbit. Launch vehicle destroyed by range safety after two minutes. Search for spacecraft has been unsuccessful.
ATS-IV (ATS D)	Aug. 10, 1968	Atlas-Centaur	Applications and Technology: To perform communication, meteorological, technology and science experiments. Gravity gradient experiment could not be conducted because spacecraft did not separate from Centaur.
INTELSAT III F-1 NON-NASA Mission	Sept. 19, 1968	Delta	Communications: Third generation Comsat commercial satellite. Improved long-tank Thor Delta destroyed itself one minute, eight seconds into the mission. Control system failure.
BIOSATELLITE III (BIOS-D)	June 28, 1969	Delta	Biology: The spacecraft completed 8-1/2 days in orbit with all subsystems performing well with the exception of the visumotor (VM) task logic of the psychomotor test panel and the JPL urine analysis sytem. Monkey onboard expired. Autopsy performed July 8. Information received to date leads to the conclusion that the animal died of a heart attack brought on by problems associated with weightlessness and a lower than normal body temperature.

We Never Went To The Moon

NAME	LAUNCH	VEHICLE	MISSION/REMARKS
APOLLO XI (AS-506/CSM-107/LM-5)	July 16, 1969	Saturn V	First manned lunar landing mission: Limited selenological inspection, photography, survey, evaluation and sampling of the lunar soil. Assess the capability and limitations of an astronaut and his equipment in the lunar environment. Astronauts: Neil A. Armstrong, Michael Collins, and Edwin E. Aldrin, Jr.
APOLLO XIII (AS-508/CSM-109/LM-7)	April 11, 1970	Saturn V	Third manned lunar landing attempt aborted after 56 hours GET due to loss of pressure in liquid oxygen in Service Module and the failure of fuel cells 1 and 3. Astronauts: James A. Lovell, Jr., Fred W. Haise, Jr., and John L. Swigert, Jr. Total flight time was 142 hrs. 54 min. and 44 seconds. Splashdown occurred in Pacific Ocean.
OAO-B	Nov. 30, 1970	Atlas-Centaur	To obtain moderate resolution spectrophotometric data in ultraviolet bands between 1100 and 4000A to investigate photometry of peculiar stars, the law of interstellar reddening, magnitude and intensity of Lyman-alpha red shift for nearby galaxies, spectra of emission and reflection nebulae and spectral energy distribution of normal stars, galaxies, and intergalactic media. Mission not accomplished. It did not achieve orbit.
Mariner H (8)	May 8, 1971	A-Centaur	To study the dynamic characteristics of the planet Mars from orbit for a minimum period of 90 days also to map approximately 70% of the planet. Mission was unsuccessful because of vehicle failure.
ITOS-B	Oct. 21, 1971	Delta	To provide improved operational infrared and visual observations of earth cloud cover for use in weather analysis and forecasting. NASA reimbursed by NOAA for both spacecraft and launch support. Mission failure due to vehicle second stage malfunction.
ITOS-E (NOAA)	July 16, 1973	Delta	Operational meteorological satellite to obtain global cloud-cover data both day and night for use in weather analysis and forecasting. NASA reimbursed by NOAA for both spacecraft and launch support. Mission failed due to vehicle second stage malfunction. Launched from Western Test Range.

Even a cursory scan of the above failure reports would lead one to conclude that failure in space is as common as it is in other areas of human endeavor. Thus, it becomes almost an insult to one's intelligence to be told that six lunar landing missions were absolutely perfect! In the following figure, we see that there are more than 80 critical elements in each flight. Multiplying 6 x 80 yields 480 critical operations or functions that had to be 100 percent.

What more can I say? We have seen that failure is a thread that runs continuously thru the fabric of space exploration. How can this thread suddenly disappear where Apollo is concerned? Any statistician would find this untenable from any reasonable standpoint. And from the standpoint of common sense, it is even more untenable.

THE MOON ROCKS

In 1977 I requisitioned some films from the Las Vegas

We Never Went To The Moon

Public Schools system. Among them was one describing and illustrating the work of the NASA Ceramics Laboratory. As the film progressed, it became clear that this facility would have been ideal to create the various "moon" rocks used as conclusive proof that the Apollo trips took place. Let's examine how this could have been done.

First, since no one had ever seen or handled a lunar mineral, whatever NASA chose to produce would become the standard. Second, NASA had the funds to employ top scientists to *predict* what kind of rocks and other minerals might be expected to be found on the lunar surface. These predictions would be made from extrapolations of terrestrial geology and data from Surveyor (if endeed, *these* really landed!). Finally, by combining speculations with some hard knowledge, it would not have been difficult to *transform* various types of earth rocks into lunar specimens. After all, the moon was most likely once a part of the earth and thus minerals would be quite similar. The only major differences would involve sedimentation, weathering, micro-meteor bombardment and so forth. All of these parameters would be either omitted or added to suit the best guesses. For example, there is a laboratory in Santa Barbara that specializes in extremely high-speed impact studies. They've achieved velocities of 32,000 feet per second with a two-stage projectile system. Obviously, rock specimens could be exposed to high-speed particles thus simulating small-particle-meteorite bombardment.

Now, who do you suppose NASA chooses to evaluate the "moon" rocks? You're right—the same people that did the early speculation as to what they would be like. Naturally, these academic geologists would preen and crow to find that the moon rocks were quite similar to their predictions. After all, they were *made to order*, weren't they. And it is a human characteristic to find what we are searching for.

To achieve a better understanding of the scenario proposed above, one should also consider the position of academia in American corporate life. Mark Twain understood it when he said.

"Tell me where a man gets his cornpone and I'll tell you where he gets his opinions."

We Never Went To The Moon

American universities are a direct reflection of American corporate life. Students are conditioned to take their places as cogs in the great American industrial wheel. Conformity, discipline, obediance are all essential elements of academic life. Those who fit the corporate mold best, are the most handsomely rewarded. Mavericks and rebels are not welcome. Men of the innovative intellect of Timothy Leary or Alan Watts find themselves either in prison or attached to the lunatic fringe by media edict.

Furthermore, grants and loans are given to those scholars who best respond to corporate plans. For example, at the Davis campus of the University of California, there are millions of dollars available to support a chemically-oriented agriculture system. Those who espouse an organic approach find themselves working at McDonalds to pay their lab fees.

Nowhere is this concept better illustrated than in American medical schools. Here, the major thrust is towards allopathic (drug) medicine. Little is taught concerning what we put into our bodies; the emphasis is on the "cure" of disease by attacking the symptoms with various drugs. By backtracking, we find that medical schools are supported by the major drug companies and these, in turn, are subservient to international drug cartels, joint ventures of such firms as I.G. Farben in Germany and Rockfeller interests in the U.S. An excellent reference work that describes this type of unholy alliance for public detriment may be found in "World Without Cancer" by G. E. Griffin.

So what we find is, ultimately, no real distinction between such agencies as NASA and the halls of ivy. Both receive public funding and directions to retain the status quo. And if that happens to be a given set of rules concerning lunar rocks, then so be it!

In summary, keep this thought in mind; once you have an unlimited budget and plenty of time, you can create almost any size, shape or type of fake evidence. Toy-like lunar modules, astronauts who avoid talking about moon landings, moon rocks made in the USA; it's all there for examination by anyone with an open mind. As has been said,

"To dare to say what others only dare to think, makes men martyrs or reformers."

Appendix

SUPPORTING EVIDENCE

No attempt has been made to categorize the following bits and pieces of the "jigsaw puzzle". In time, as more data is acquired from interested contributors, I will make an attempt to clearly position each piece. But for now, bear with me and place the pieces in your own mind where they fit best.

BETTY GRISSOM

Recently a supporter in Texas relayed the information that Betty Grissom's home was invaded by government agents after the death of Gus. They seized all his papers and when they were returned, nothing concerning Apollo was among them. Recall that Grissom was an outspoken critic of the entire Apollo project and there is certainly a possibility that he put his criticism in writing. His report, like Baron's 500 pager and Gen. Phillips' report to Atwood appears to have been dropped in an Orwellian "memory hole". (Readers of Orwell's novel *1984* will recall that when Big Brother didn't like certain facts, they were dropped into a memory hole to vanish forever. For an insight into the chances of success for retrieving these facts, see the letters reproduced on pages 196-198.)

THE ASTRONAUTS' SUITS

A writer of San Jose, Calif., who has authored a book on astronauts' garb, said that when he visited the suit research facility at Sunnyvale, Calif., he was shocked. He expected a huge department to be busy designing and fabricating the critical space suit; instead, one man with a few employees had total charge of the project. The supervisor said that "it would put the Russian space program back several years if the U.S. divulged their space suit secrets."

A FORMER NASA EMPLOYEE SPEAKS

After appearing on KGO radio, I received many letters; one from a former Apollo project engineer commented that as soon as he reported for work at a site in Alabama, he sensed the project was a hoax. Several other former space project technical personnel have made the same comment. (I would like to hear from others).

THE INTELLIGENCE PYRAMID

Few people realize just how large the U.S. spy and security organization is. Here is what we are up against when seeking the truth; CIA, 20,000 people, $800 million budget, NSA, 20,000, 1.2 billion, FBI, 24,000, 513 million, DIA, 4,300, 200 million, military intelligence, no figures available. Many other departments (State, Treasury, Energy, etc.) have their own intelligence groups. It is obvious that if the Feds want to hide something, they have the people and they have your money to do it.

MASSIVE ORGANIZATIONAL CAPABILITY

Few people realize the power of the establishment. But it becomes plainly visible when one realizes that ALL manufactures are party to the new "product identification code" that appears on virtually everything sold. The next step will be to put a PIC on *you* so that no one can buy or sell without being identified without doubt.

MEDIA OPPOSITION

With few exceptions, it has been very difficult to get the moon hoax message into print. TV and radio are relatively easy but there appears to be a seamless facade where print media is concerned. No major publisher will touch my book.

We are told that we have the best diet in the world. If so, why do Americans rank 23rd in longevity? Salem Kirban in his latest books cites the fact that 90 percent of the food purchased in a supermarket was bought because of a lie. Everyone of us ingests five pounds of food additives a year. The rate of deaths due to cancer is almost exactly that of the rate of increase of chemical additions to food. So it appears that the myth of a well-fed America emerges in the hard statistics of a sick America.

Dr. Martin Larson of Phoenix Az, cites the fact that the Internal Revenue Service operates on 99 percent bluff. For example, although you must answer the summons to bring your records to an IRS audit, under the privilege of the Fourth Amendment (privacy of person, property and papers) you don't have to show them. The IRS even admits this in their own Special Agents Handbook. So tax collection, while an ongoing swindle of the American people is also a hoax.

And we all sense in our inner selves that the oil shortage is a hoax . . . I recently flew to California with a Montanan who said that many capped oil wells exist in Wyoming . . . he actually saw them. And recently it was revealed that most of the Alaskan oil is going to Japan at high prices.

An innovative doctor in California was recently jailed for trying to cure his patients with other than the "cut-burn-poison" treatment approved by the AMA for cancer victims. Ivan Illich in his book MEDICAL NEMESIS, points out that we live in a dark age of medicine where physicians often do more harm than good. So medical treatment appears to be another American hoax.

And the list could go on . . . our point is this. We have been boondoggled and misled for many decades. But as Lincoln said, you cannot fool all of the people all of the time.

My feelings about Apollo is that it is a hoax for no other reason than the government is a specialist in hoaxing the public.

THE ASTRONAUTS

In 1977 I was invited to appear on CBS Television to debate with Col. Edwin "Buzz" Aldrin. The moderator was Truman Lafayette who was anxious to prove, once and for all, that my contentions were either right or wrong. But

Aldrin didn't show up and I did the show alone. At the end I addressed Col. Aldrin saying that since about 25 percent of the American people doubt the moon landings were made, it was his obligation as a man and public servant to defend his case in person. I am willing to debate any or all of the astronauts at any time on live TV or in person anywhere.

Neil Armstrong has just about gone underground. He will not speak on the phone to me or to my co-investigators. His secretary answers letters with a polite refusal to comment. His only appearances these days are in behalf of bankrupt car companies.

Astronaut Irving's mother berated me on radio when I appeared on the Jim Eason show in San Francisco. But when I offered to debate her son on the same program, there was a dead silence.

How many people have said that the astronauts do not want to dignify my claims with a public response. But my claims are not what is relevant . . . it is the contention of more than a fourth of the American people that the moon landings were faked!! David Wise, in his book *"The Politics Of Lying"* states that an informal poll by a newspaper chain in the Southeast U.S., revealed that about that percentage of Americans do not believe the astronauts are telling the truth! Surely when millions of people doubt a small segment of our population, it is up to them to answer in public debate. But so far, silence. I theorize that the astronauts are afraid to talk because of the new technique of Psychological Stress Evaluation. This electronic method allows the investigator to detect stresses in the voice patterns of the speaker indicating truth or lies. I suggest that readers try to interview astronauts and record their voices. Then, at a later time, subject the recordings to PSE. Better yet, engage the astronauts in live conversation with a PSE monitor operating nearby. This would be a great project for an investigative reporter of a large metropolitan daily or TV news staff.

THOMAS RONALD BARON

Thinking back to 1974, I realize that it was a man, Tom Baron, who focused my thoughts and made me realize that the moon hoax was not only possible but more than likely.

Baron was an employee of North American Aviation assigned to Pad 34, Cape Canaveral. He maintained a log of events for a year and a half prior to the deaths of Grissom, Chafee and White in January of 1967. As you will recall, the three astronauts were burned to death in their command capsule atop a rocket on Pad 34.

During the investigation which followed this tragedy, Baron came forth voluntarily and testified to the gross mismanagement and ineptitude of both NAA and NASA. Significantly, his report was almost identical to that of General Sam Phillips, boss of the Apollo project. Phillips submitted a report to J. Atwood, President of NAA, in 1966 describing in detail the many failures of Apollo and his own disillusionment with the progress of the effort.

So we have an Air Force General and an employee of NAA agreeing that the Apollo project was in sad shape prior to the catastrophe. Baron was found crushed to death in his car four days after he testified. Phillips went on to another job . . . head of a security agency. End of investigation.

Now most of us recall that following the assassination of Kennedy, 18 witnesses who had something to contribute were found dead after mysterious happenings. In 1967, following the deaths of the astronauts, four other Apollo pilots died in accidents . . . Williams in a mid-air explosion, two in a routine jet landing, ex-combat pilot Given in a one-car accident in Texas. No astronauts have died since. Odd, in my opinion. And particularly odd in Grissom's case. He had often given unauthorized statements to the press regarding his displeasure with Apollo. Once he is said to have hung a lemon on the command capsule to indicate his lack of confidence. From events that ensued, his suspicions were justified.

So it was Thomas Ronald Baron who triggered my serious investigation . . . one which has continued to this very day. I think of his sacrafice as being parallel to that of John Brown . . . a willingness to put his life and fortunes on the line for his principles. I consider Baron as an unsung hero in mankind's struggle for truth.

We Never Went To The Moon

NOTE TO READERS

As you read the following material, I don't ask you to believe me . . . only keep an open mind. I once had a qualified belief that men landed on the moon. But when evidence to the contrary built up, I changed my mind.

Investigations of this nature are similar to putting together a jigsaw puzzle. No single piece can give you the whole picture but as you begin to assemble the pieces, a logical picture begins to appear. Each piece (of evidence) adds to the completeness.

I have, by no means, assembled the complete picture, but the pieces gathered to date seem to indicate that we did not go to the moon. So consider the following as pieces of a puzzle and form your own opinion.

OTHER HOAXES AS SUPPORTING EVIDENCE

In 1944 I was commander of a company of naval officer candidates preparing for the invasion of Japan. One of my men was particularly intelligent and many of the statements he made at that time have come true. For example, he advised me never to save money but to spend it having a good time. He predicted that those who put money aside would one day find it worthless. Certainly those who have painstakingly saved for their retirement find their money almost worthless. So what he predicted has come true . . . a hoax on the American people with regard to money. It is a known fact that U.S. Savings Bonds actually lose value over the years.

THE MINNEAPOLIS DOCTOR

A fellow believer in the moon hoax, this doctor contends that the face shields of the astronauts could not withstand the extreme temperature differentials on the moon. As you probably know, temperatures vary from 200 to 300 plus to an equivalent amount below zero! I checked this with an airline pilot who agreed; he said that it required very careful regulation of the windshield temperature to prevent cracking when descending from high altitudes.

NO CRATERS

In all NASA animation of lunar flights, there is shown craters being created below the lunar landing module by the jet blast of the landing engine. In every official NASA photo of the lunar landing module on the moon, there are not craters. In fact, the surface looks completely undisturbed!!! Check this out for yourself in your local library. If you can find a picture showing a crater, please send it to me or give me the index number.

NO DUST

When Apollo II was allegedly landing on the moon, we hear a voice say . . . "picking up a little dust." Had this dust arisen, it would have covered various articles on the moon after landing. But there is no evidence of this particularly on the face shields.

LIGHTING

In the famous picture of Col. Aldrin taken by Armstrong, the former is standing with his back to the sun. Instead of his front being in deep shadow, it is brightly illuminated. What is the source of the light? And if there is a source, it would show in the reflection from Aldrin's face shield. Again, check this out in your local library in pictures of the moon landings. Many pictures show this same anomaly.

I once asked a CBS TV lighting engineer about this particular photo and he said that it would require all his skill and equipment to duplicate this shot and would have taken three or four hours to light.

CHUCK ASHMAN

I have found that the standard procedure for discrediting someone is to impugn their background. In December of 1975, I received a call from Chuck Ashman who wanted me to talk on his radio show. Just prior to my phone-interview, he called me and said that he had talked with my former employers at Rocketdyne. Both the VP and head of public relations told Ashman that I had been fired and was therefore merely a disgruntled employee with an ax to grind. I was not fired and have letters to prove it from Rocketdyn'es personnel department. During my talk with Ashman, he cut me off the air suddenly saying that I was an example of someone involved with irresponsible journalism.

BARON'S DEATH

Tom Baron was not autopsied despite a state law in Florida to the contrary. A friend contends that he was drugged and then placed in his car and driven to scene of his "accidental" death. Inquiries regarding Baron's death and his reports meet with the same blank wall. Try it yourself for further proof.

LUNAR GRAVITY

An engineer from Seattle wrote to say that the figures on lunar gravity are erroneous. I have always felt that if a serious engineering effort were implemented and the data now restricted from public view exposed, that it would not be difficult to prove the moon flights were faked, but the problem is this: NASA will not release actual Apollo flight data.

DAVID HUNTSMAN

After appearing on a phone interview with Tom Snyder in NY, I received a lot of calls and letters. One was from a Dave Huntsman of the Houston Space Center. He said he would fly out to see me since he didn't want to continue to work with the astronauts if they proved out to be liars. So he flew to Santa Cruz to see my manuscript. His mother accompanied him. Both seemed quite nervous. I gave him some material and he left. I learned later that he was employed by Niel Armstrong, allegedly Number One on the moon. Strange . . . and I cannot figure it out to this day.

JIM OBERG

Another Houston man and part-timer at the Space Center. I wrote a number of times to critique my theory. Later, a correspondent in NY told me that Oberg had called me a nut and poorly informed. The correspondent also said that Oberg was a CIA employee. Again, a strange event that defies reduction to simple terms.

CACTUS SPRINGS

I talked with a woman in Nevada who said that two NASA engineers told her the moon flights were faked. I left immediately to interview her in person in Sparks NV. When I arrived she denied having said anything and two police threatened to arrest my wife and I because we had "threatened the woman."

KOME

In December of 1975 I was invited to appear on radio station KOME in San Jose Calif. The moderator was Victor Boc. About half-way thru the three hour show, we were off the air due to someone having bombed the transmitter from the air with a flammable substance. I appeared several weeks later while the remote transmitter was guarded by armed personnel of the station. Later, KOME staff claim that only a relay went out. Who has the power to order aircraft to bomb radio transmitters? You tell me?

CAPSULE RETURN

During a broadcast, an airline pilot phoned to tell me that he had once observed a command capsule being dropped from a high-flying plane. The chutes opened and it continued its descent as the pilot flew on to Japan. This correlates with my contention that the astronauts were "returned" by being placed in a heat-streaked capsule and dropped from an unmarked air force plane in the pickup zone.

THE PHONE CALL

During a talk show on KRIZ in Phoenix, a man phoned in to say that he was a member of Army intelligence during the Apollo project and that I was right . . . THE FLIGHTS WERE FAKED. He said that the deaths of other astronauts was squelched by NASA.

THE ELECTRONICS EXPERT

A radio expert called during a show and said that he believed my story since all transmissions to and from the "astronauts" were done at the gigahertz level thus making it impossible for hams to verify any lunar broadcasts. Another expert told me that NASA launched a TETRA satellite in the spring of 1969 which emitted the same frequencies as a command capsule would have done. It circled the earth until after the last "flight".

LLOYD MALLAN

An expert space scientist and photographer wrote a series of articles for Science and Mechanics in 1966 in which he proved that the Russian space exploits were faked. Lloyd died of cancer in 1972 with no comment on the Apollo project.

PAUL JACOBS

In 1978, the famous investigative journalist, Paul Jacobs of San Francisco agreed to help me. He went to Washington DC and interrogated the head of the U.S. Geological Survey Department regarding his views on the moon landings. The bureau chief gave cryptic answers according to Paul. Paul and his wife died suddenly of cancer in mid-78.

THE DISMANTLED PLANE

While in Las Vegas in 1976, I met a man who told me the following story which he claimed was true. It seems a doctor and his family accidentally flew over the secret DOE (former-ly NTS) base north of Vegas. The base is definitely off-limits to both air and surface travel. It is also the region that I claim was used for "lunar" photography. The doctor's plane was forced down by USAF fighter planes and was totally disman-tled . . . evidently searching for a hidden camera. The doctor and his family were questioned at great length and finally released. The plane was shipped back to the doctor in pieces.

Last fall (late 1979) I asked for permission to fly my own plane over. A segment spokesman warned me that I, too, would be forced down and asked some very searching questions. Try it yourself sometime for further proof.

VISUAL EVIDENCE

Recently, a young woman acquaintance of mine commented on my first version of WE NEVER WENT TO THE MOON.

"I think you're right Bill . . . I don't think we ever went to the moon."

"Why do you say that?"

"Not enough visual evidence."

This is exactly in agreement with the contention that NASA could have easily produced irrefutable visual evidence that astronauts did, indeed, land on the lunar surface.

Here are some of the methods that could have been used:

1. A quantity of lightweight black or colored powder could have been transported to the moon instead of some of the experimental equipment. This powder could have been scattered by hand or a lawn spreader to make a recognizable pattern easily seen by telescopes or even binoculars on earth. Astronomers say that items about ½ mile in diameter would be visible through a telescope. Thus, a series of concentric circles created by the powder would have provided evidence of moon landings forever.

2. The Echo satellite was launched in the mid-fifties. It consisted of an aluminized mylar baloon with a filling of nitrogen gas. It was launched within a small container, inflated in the vacuum of space and circled the earth for several months always plainly visible with the naked eye.

   This same principle could have been easily adapted to making the lunar landings credible. For example, a large envelope of aluminized mylar could have been fabricated on earth and inflated with a pressurized gas by the astronauts. To avoid having to take an envelope of giant dimensions, a number of smaller envelopes could have been used by arranging them in checkerboard fashion. By placing a sufficient number of these in position, the pattern could have been seen by earthlings without major optical aids!

3. The lunar lander employed a rocket engine burning nitrogen tetroxide and unsymmetrical dimethyl hydrazine. These propellants are hypergolic which means that they ignite on contact. The astronauts could have left a timer on the lunar lander whick would have opened the valves of the propellant tanks after they left the scene. The burning of these propellants plus the dust cloud raised by the jet blast might have been visible from the earth. Alternatively, the propellants might have been combined explosively with even greater effect. Placing them below the surface could have prouded a giant cloud of moon dust which might have been detectable from earth.

4. There is allegedly a laser reflector on the moon to which a laser beam is transmitted from observatories on earth. To date I have been unable to find anyone who has had any *direct contact* with this experiment. Further, the laser reflector, if it does exist could have been planted on the moon by an unmanned vehicle. The point I am trying to make is that instead of hauling the 600 pound Lunar Rover to the moon several times, the astronauts could have taken a laser beam device to send a laser beam back to earth so that the average citizen would be able to see it.

Mylar, chemical clouds, laser beams are only a few of the many ways that the astronauts could have provided some real, tangible, irrefutable proof that men had landed on the lunar surface. The fact that NONE of these methods was employed indicates that NASA either didn't feel that they were necessary for proof or that they simply could not do it because the trips were simulated. It is the latter possibility that seems strongest to many people.

QUARANTINE

To protect the people of earth from lunar germs, the astronauts were held in strict quarantine for about 18 days after their alleged return to earth. After the return of the Apollo 11 crew, Collins, Armstrong and Aldrin, there was no mention of any bacteria, germs or other life found on the moon. If this was the case, then why was it necessary to quarantine the remaining Apollo crews?

It is appropriate to add here that a government which cares so little for its people as to allow the sale of junk foods loaded with lethal preservatives, tobacco and other harmful substances, would really not be all that concerned about lunar germs.

HIGH LEVEL SOUND

NASA has distributed a record which allegedly presents the actual sounds of the Apollo 11 flight. In it we hear Armstrong and Aldrin talking with the Mission Control staff at Houston *while they are descending* to the surface of the moon.

There is just one problem . . . talking near a rocket engine developing 10,000 lbs of thrust would be impossible since the sound level of this engine is in the area of 140 to 150 db. Voices could not be heard no matter what kind of amplification was used.

APOLLO SIX

A review of most of the current books on the moon project reveals that the Apollo 6 flight is either not mentioned or is quickly glossed over. Why?

Apollo Six was, by even NASA's standards a *total disaster*. The second stage did not light and there were over 20 major failures in the flight. Apollo Six was intended to "Man-rate" the Saturn Five vehicle and this it did *not* do. However Apollo Seven was by NASA's declaration, "perfect" and is highly touted in the literature.

Could it be that Apollo Six was the last flight to be honestly reported? Statisticians will state that it is not possible for a failure-ridden device to suddenly cure itself of its mechanical ills.

APOLLO RECORDS

It is impossible for the layman investigator to obtain technical records of the Apollo project. This was discovered when the author wrote a letter to Rocketdyne's head of publication, James McCafferty. Jim replied that Apollo records, "while not classified, are not available to the public." It is curious that a peaceful mission's records are hidden. We can only ask, why?

THE TTS SATELLITES

NASA launched a series of Apollo Tracking Network Test and Training Satellites (TTS) in the TETR series which transmitted signals just like Apollo capsules (for practice of course). It is interesting to note that TETR-C was launched in 1969 and orbited the earth until 1974. Could it be that ALL transmissions from the moon came from the TETR satellite?

NINE DAYS IN SPACE . . .

In June 1969, a Biosatellite was launched which proved that monkeys could not survive more than nine days in space. If conditions in space are lethal for monkeys, it is likely that they would be lethal for humans also.

Note that Apollo 17 lasted 12 days.

THE UNMANNED LM

In 1967, following the death of the three astronauts on Pad 34, a report was issued by the Subcommittee on NASA Oversight of the Committee on Science and Astronautics, U.S. House of Representatives, Ninetieth Congress. On page 591 of Volume I there is the following quote:

We Never Went To The Moon

"UNMANNED LM: THE PANEL WAS PERSUADED THAT THERE WERE PLAUSIBLE CONTINGENCIES WHICH WOULD INDICATE THE DESIRABILITY OF USING AN UNMANNED LM for the first lunar landing and recommended the development of a plan directed at making an unmanned lunar landing LEM capability available in a timely manner should it be necessary."

It is curious that there was no mention of this made and that further publicity as to an unmanned landing was *not* released to the public.

MOON ROCKS

There are three major pieces of evidence that NASA has provided to prove their moon flights:

1. Photographs, still and motion, silent and sound
2. Moon rocks
3. The testimony of the astronauts

Obviously, pictures can be faked and the words of the astronauts could have been purchased. But what about the rooks?

NASA has a facility to manufacture ceramics. To do this requires a high temperature furnace. Various minerals could have been combined to creat a credible supply of "moon rocks". Furthermore, when there are no other samples to compare them to, it is logical that the rocks furnished NASA would simply stand on their own "merits".

An interesting sidelight . . . Paul Jacobs, the famous investigative journalist went to Washington to search for the Baron report (more on this shortly). While there, he interviewed the chief U.S. geologist. He asked him if the moon rocks were real. The geologist replied that they were. Paul then said . . .

"If they were not real and you were in on the hoax, you would attest to their reality wouldn't you?"

The geologist did not answer . . . he just smiled.

We Never Went To The Moon

MOON PHOTO LIGHTING

In several of the photographs allegedly taken on the moon there are striking anomalies. For instance, in the photo of Col. Aldrin taken by Armstrong, there is a strong backlighting effect by the sun. And yet Aldrin's front is also illuminated. If Armstrong had provided the light source, flash or flood, it would have been reflected in Aldrin's helmet faceplate. And yet there is no trace of artifical light showing in the faceplate. Why?

This curious contradiction occurs in several other photos of Apollo 11 as well as in the other Apollo flight photo records.

LACK OF STARS

The astronauts had a golden opportunity to take magnificent photographs of the stars since there was not atmosphere on the moon to restrict or diffuse their light. And yet there is only one dim, somewhat blurred photo of stars taken with ultra-violet light sensitive film. Instead of taking the 600 pound Lunar Rover on three flights, a compact, 600 pound astronomical telescope with suitable film could have been taken, thus assuring earthbound scientists of the best views of stellar bodies obtained to date.

NEIL ARMSTRONG

During a phone-in broadcast from Chicago, the moderator, Warren Frieberg, was initially somewhat hostile to my story. Then he became curiously silent. "Perhaps you're right, Bill," he said, "I just recalled that Armstrong has only granted three interviews since he went into semi-retirement. It seems to me that a world-famous astronaut would make himself more available to the scientific and lay community."

Armstrong is almost impossible to reach. His communications are handled by a public relations firm in NY. Once, in a conversation with Dave Develo, a TV talk show MC, Armstrong parried questions never once answering them with any degree of accuracy or candor.

TEMPERATURES ON THE MOON

There is no atmosphere to shield the lunar surface from the sun's rays. As a result, temperatures on the moon are in excess of 250 F during the lunar day. During lunar night, the lack of atmosphere causes the temperature to drop to below - 250 F. This also occurs to a lesser degree in the shaded portions of the moon's surface.

The simple shielding of the astronauts' space suits would not have provided protection against these temperature extremes.

COSMIC AND SOLAR RADIATION

In the early fifties, the Russian scientists proved to their own satisfaction that the surface of the moon would be lethal to humans. As a result, they decided at that time they would not push manned landings. The space "race" existed, therefore, only in the public relations office of NASA. The race was synthesized to appropriate funds from the treasury. As one commentator said, "NASA has one hand grasping for the moon and the other in the taxpayer's pocket."

SUMMARY, CONCLUSIONS AND RECOMMENDATIONS

Thomas Carlyle once said,

> "Go as far as you can see. When you get there, you will be able to see further."

That's the present position of the moon hoax investigation. To bring it to a successful conclusion will require the work of many people. I ask everyone who reads these words to contribute what they can, either in funds or data. I am certain that the investigation will ultimately be successful and here's why:

There are many methods of communication in the universe. We have all had experiences of KNOWING something without knowing just why. I believe that the 20 to 30 percent of the U.S. population that KNOWS we didn't land men on the moon, know this because of some unexplained method of communication. When millions of people are certain of a single fact, just the sheer weight of numbers gives credibility. But beyond that are the many unanswered questions . . . the list is almost endless.

1. Why didn't the astronauts make some visible signal on the moon? Instead of hauling the lunar rover up, the same weight in a lightweight black dust would have left a visible symbol on the moon's surface.

2. Why were the astronauts held in quarantine so long? The U.S. normally doesn't concern itself with our health (ie, nuclear power, junk foods, swine flu shots) so why would they repeatedly quarantine the astronauts when it had been proven on the first "mission" that the moon was sterile? A psychologist friends says that they would not have been able to hold up under questioning so soon after their charade.

3. Why was Capricorn I made to show an ostensible faked landing on the planet Mars? Was it to avoid confrontation with the facts of the moon hoax?

4. Why was the fact that Apollo was a military project hidden from the public?

5. Why was there never a mention of gold, silver or precious stones? Surely had the trips been made there would have been some discovery . . . or non-discovery.

6. Why did the press not mention that the astronauts were training at NTS?

7. Why did the Dutch papers question the lunar landings in July of 1969 and why was this not reported in the U.S. press.

8. Why did Wally Shirra say in February of 1966, "I doubt if I could have flown my (Mercury and Gemini) missions if they had encountered as many foul-ups as the Apollo craft"?

9. Why did Howard Benedict of Associated Press say in 1966, "Nothing appeared to be going right. Rockets blew up in tests, there were troubles with the Apollo spacecraft. Schedules slipped badly. Some people feel that the Apollo

project is falling apart at the seams."

Personally, the moon hoax is just one of many that I have observed in my nearly six decades in America. I love this country and its people but I have grave doubts about its government . . . I consider it to be Public Enemy Number 1. I'll leave you with my own philosophy . . .

Question (and Challenge) Authority!

Bill Kaysing
1994

Space Division
Rockwell International

12214 Lakewood Boulevard
Downey, California 90241

October 27, 1975

Mr. Bill Kaysing
146 Palo Verde Terrace
Santa Cruz, CA 95060

Dear Mr. Kaysing:

We are aware of the report authored by Thomas Baron
in the spring of 1967 and at that time did read a copy,
but did not retain it for our files.

It is our understanding at that time that there were
limited copies printed by a printing firm in Cocoa Beach,
Fla., which has since gone out of business.

We neither have a copy of the referenced report, nor
do we have any idea on how to obtain one.

Sincerely,

Richard E. Barton

Richard E. Barton
Director
Public Relations

/ss

---

*Doesn't it seem somewhat strange and curious that the company with
the prime contract for Apollo would discard such a damning report as that
prepared by the now-deceased Thomas R. Baron? At least they could have
retained a copy for future reference on how not to conduct a lunar landing
operation.*

United States Senate

COMMITTEE ON THE BUDGET
WASHINGTON, D.C. 20510

December 15, 1975

Bill Kaysing
146 Palo Verde Terrace
Santa Cruz, CA   95060

Dear Mr. Kaysing:

Thank you for your recent request for a copy of the Thomas R. Baron Report.

The reason I sent you a copy of the hearings rather than a copy of the Baron Report is because I have been unable to locate a copy of the report. It seems that none of the agencies involved have copies of the report to date. Also it is my understanding that Mr. Baron is dead and no one knows where to obtain any more copies.

If there is anyhting else I can do to be of assistance please do not hesitate to call on me.

Best wishes for the holiday season,

Sincerely,

Walter F. Mondale

A future vice president of the United States was unable to help the author find a copy of the crucial and damning Baron report.

We Never Went To The Moon

DEPARTMENT OF THE AIR FORCE
HEADQUARTERS SPACE DIVISION (AFSC)
LOS ANGELES AIR FORCE STATION, PO BOX 92960, WORLDWAY POSTAL CENTER
LOS ANGELES, CA 90009

8 Jan 1981

Mr Peter Barry
2932 Old San Jose Rd
Soquel, CA   95073

Dear Mr Barry

Your letter to the USAF Public Information Office in Washington, D.C.
was forwarded to this office for reply.

I regret that we are unable to furnish you a copy of the report General
Phillips sent to Mr Atwood of North American Aviation in the fall of
1966.

Beginning January 1964, General Sam Phillips was on detached service
from the U. S. Air Force to the National Aeronautics and Space Administration as Director of the United States Apollo Lunar Landing Program
and remained in this position until September 1969.

I would like to suggest that you contact the National Aeronautics and
Space Administration and they perhaps can provide you with the information you requested.   Their address follows:

> Mr Brian Duff
> Director of Public Affairs
> NASA Headquarters
> Washington, D C 20546

Sincerely

HERBERT G. BAKER, Major, USAF
Director of Public Affairs

---

*Typical of the type of letter that one receives from government
bureaucracies, this one demonstrates that important evidence is either with-
held or has been dropped into an Orwellian "memory hole". Surely, an
important report like the one that Phillips wrote to Atwood about the repeated failures of the Apollo project would be retained in Air Force archives
and should be available to the public. It is not classified but is of great
historical importance.*

Bibliography

Hot War On The Consumer	David Sanford, Pitman - New Republic
Apollo On The Moon	H.S. Cooper, Dial Press
Project Apollo	Tom Alexander, Harper Row
Journey To Tranquility	Silcock Dunn, Doubleday
Mission To The Moon	Kennan Harvey, Morrow
Stanley Kubrick Driects	Walker, Harcourt Brace
Space	Moore, Natural History
Write Me In	Gregory, Bantam
Return To Earth	Aldrin, Random House
Man On The Moon	Mansfield, Stein Day
The Decision To Go To The Moon	Logsdon, MIT Press
Space Travel	Gartmann, Viking Press
A Heritage Of Stone	Garrison, Putnam
Picture History Rockets	Akens, Strode
History of Rocketry - Space Travel	Von Braun, Corwell
First On The Moon	Armstrong - Collins - Aldrin, Littel Brown
Earthbound Astronauts	Lay, Prentice Hall
Moon Flight Atlas	Moore, Rand McNally

The End!

Made in the USA
Monee, IL
06 April 2025

15270176R00116